# CREATIVE RECYCLING
## IN EMBROIDERY

# CREATIVE RECYCLING

## IN EMBROIDERY

## VAL HOLMES

BATSFORD

*Previous page:* Carnet de
Vogage. *Bus pass stitched by*
*Fanny Violet with images of*
*London city life.*

First published in the United Kingdom in 2006 by
Batsford
151 Freston Road
London
W10 6TH

An imprint of Anova Books Company Ltd

ISBN-13: 9 780713 489866
ISBN-10: 0 7134 8986 3

A CIP catalogue record for this book is available from the British Library.

10 9 8 7 6 5 4 3 2 1

Reproduction by Classicscan, Singapore
Printed and bound by WKT Co Ltd, China

This book can be ordered direct from the publisher at the website:
www.anovabooks.com, or try your local bookshop

Distributed in the United States and Canada by Sterling Publishing Co.,
387 Park Avenue South, New York, NY 10016, USA

# Contents

# INTRODUCTION

Recycling objects and images has been a part of avant-garde art practice since Marcel Duchamp's found objects of the early 20th century. In the 21st century this is now part of a major wave in contemporary art, and rather than just jumping in on a fashion bandwagon, it's probably a good idea to look at this phenomenon and try to assess what recycling can bring to our work before embarking on our own interpretations.

## WHY RECYCLE?

The inclusion of significant objects in a piece of work can be used to add meaning. These objects may be of a personal nature and give the work a notion of a personal history or diary, a life lived, or the memory of a particular experience or person. The objects included may be of a more general nature and could create relationships between the viewer and the piece of work as the viewer recognizes objects that are part of their own experience.

### INCLUDING FRAGILE ITEMS

Most notably, organic objects or old worn fabrics can be included, or papers that may have a limited life expectancy; the work is therefore fragile and ephemeral as well. The notion of art values comes into play here, as 'collectable' art, which has a value, is necessarily conservable. Work with a short life expectancy turns this old art market concept on its head. This is already a well-worn idea, but as we still face collectable art at an uncollectable price (even with museum budgets) it's still worth doing. Why can't we accept the notion that a piece of art has just the value of the price ticket attached to it, and it is purchased because it is wanted at that instant – just like a coat. Also, just like a coat, it may not always have the same value or inspire the same desire, and may even wear out just the same.

### REUSING EXISTING PIECES OF EMBROIDERY

*Right: Bag by Mary Crehan. Recycled wrapping woven into layers of netting from orange and lemon bags.*

Reworking old embroideries may just be a way of coming to terms with a piece that 'failed'; finding a way to make it come together some time later can be very satisfying, even if it means cutting it up into little pieces! Incorporating found ethnic embroideries into work for cross-cultural reference needs to be

6

done with respect for the culture concerned. Including old family embroideries in work can, again, be a way of bringing personal histories into your work.

## RECYCLING WASTE

Recycling waste as a policy or politic can be used as a comment on a waste-producing society, and the need for a politic on recycling. Recycling in art is very often an expression of our over-consumer society, where everything is short lived and throwaway, to the detriment of the planet, our own pockets and peace of mind, as we constantly run after the latest gadget or technique that will bring us paradise. Recycling and reusing can be a comment on consumerism.

## FOR ECONOMY OR AS AN ANTITHESIS TO 'NORMAL' EMBROIDERY

The rich embellishment of surfaces has throughout history been used to give a sense of luxury and worth to objects and households. The longevity of textile objects and notion of conservation and value can be undermined by the recycling of worthless or ephemeral objects. Recycling can comment on these established value judgements attributed to embroidery.

For recycling to work in 'art', I feel there has to be a reasoning behind the choice of using the recycled material for it to bring something extra to the work itself otherwise the textile piece could simply be created on a 'normal' surface with new materials. For recycling to work as part of a 'textile' process, the objects recycled will be chosen for the textures and surfaces that can be achieved through using them. In the following chapters, we are going to look at different types of materials and how they can be incorporated and recycled into embroidery and textile art pieces.

# CHAPTER ONE
# RECYCLING FIBRE WASTE

## WORKING WITH SILK

Silk is such a beautiful fibre, with its natural qualities of brilliance and drape. It is not surprising that it is prized by all those who use it in whatever shape or form. It adds a note of luxury and intrinsic richness to any work; by the effects that it brings; but also as a cultural and historical statement – silk has always been a fabric of the wealthy and noble classes.

In the following pages we look at ways of using silk fibres and waste to create surfaces for embroidery.

### SILK THROWSTER'S WASTE ON AQUABOND OR DISSOLVABLE FABRIC AS A SURFACE FOR EMBROIDERY

Silk throwster's waste is left over from the spinning of fine fibres for silk production. These fibres are of varying thickness, soft or sometimes knotted. They make interesting textures and surfaces when stitched together.

Aquabond is a strong vanishing fabric similar to Solusheet, but presented on a paper backing, as one side of this fabric is sticky. Waste fabrics, fibres or threads can be positioned on this fabric, once the paper backing is removed, and they will be held in place while being stitched. It is the best fabric to use for this experiment as the fibres are held firmly in place as you stitch, and stick less around the needle.

If you find the stickiness of any exposed Aquabond disagreeable, you can place a fine film of Aquafilm plastic dissolvable over the surface before putting the work in an embroidery hoop, but this isn't really necessary.

*Below:* Vignes dans le Corbière. *The base of this hanging is worked with fleece stitch over silk throwster's waste.*

### Ideas

- Arrange the silk throwster's waste over the surface of the Aquabond, taking into consideration the different textures available, and keeping the work light and airy to create a lacy structure.
- Stitching with fleece stitch in similar colours will hold the silk waste together and the stitching will hardly show, becoming almost part of the fibre structure itself. You can further adorn the work as you wish, but the fibres will hold together. You could also use an invisible thread for this first holding stitching.
- Long straight-stitch blocks or colouring in will also hold the surface together and will allow you to add colour and movement to your work.

### Tension techniques

- Fleece stitch can be rather attractive worked with a whip stitch cord, although this will add weight to the lines.
- Colouring in can be attractive with short, sharp, to-and-fro movements, using a feather stitch for added colour along the stitched lines, and particularly where the direction of the stitching changes backwards and forwards.

*Above: Sketchbook image of vines in the* corbière.

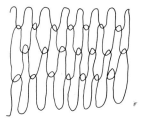

*Above: Fleece stitch design to be worked with free machine embroidery.*

*Left: Detail of* Vignes dans le Corbière, *showing the work in throwster's waste with fleece stitch in a variegated thread. The lightweight watercolour on the textured watercolour paper on the original painting influenced the choice of medium for the embroidery.*

## SILK TOPS AND AQUABOND WITH INCORPORATED FLOWERS AND PETALS

Silk tops are soft, fine fibres of equal thickness that are often presented dyed and ready for use. They are long, silk fibres that have been prepared by machine and carded ready for spinning and weaving.

### Technique

1. Pull these fibres out from the packet rather than cut them so that they already form a surface with tensile strength.
2. Arrange them on the sticky surface of the Aquabond. This can be in straight lines, crossed or curled onto the surface.
3. As the fibres are already long, the stitching required to hold them together can be quite light, and a vermicelli stitch that doesn't even cross over can be used, as there will already be some crossing of the silk fibres.
4. You may include dried flower petals or skeleton leaves into the surface while stitching lightly with a vermicelli stitch.
5. This surface can also be hand stitched; the quality of the silk fibres, with petals or other organic material added, will be quite firm. As long as the hand stitching is sufficient and relatively continuous this surface will hold together.

*Right:* Doesn't Take Much to Tear Us into Pieces *(detail). The silk tops were placed on Aquabond with hydrangea petals, and stitched with a vermicelli stitch in a slightly tight top tension and gold thread in the bobbin. Skeleton leaves were torn and attached afterwards by hand.*

- If you do not have any Aquabond, other vanishing fabrics can be used for either of these experiments. The waste threads can simply be placed onto Solusheet and stitched into place.
- Use a cocktail stick to guide the threads into place as you stitch if you need to.
- Throwster's waste still contains an element of silk gum, so stitch slowly or the fibres will tend to stick around the needle. Once the surface is held down lightly you will be able to stitch more quickly if you want to add further embroidery.
- The fibres can also be sandwiched between two layers of Aquafilm dissolvable fabric instead of being placed onto Aquabond.

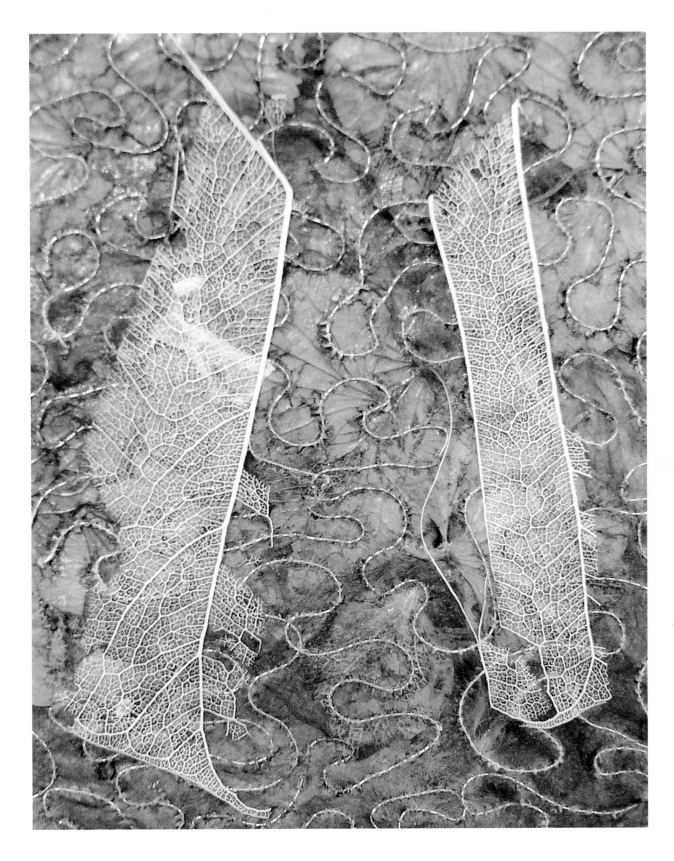

## SILK 'PAPER' WITH INCORPORATED BITS AND PIECES

Technically there is no such thing as silk paper. Paper is made from pure cellulose fibres, which form a natural glue and stick together to form a paper surface. However, a technique has been developed to make 'silk paper' from silk tops or other fibres.

### You will need:
- A plastic sheet or cling film (san wrap)
- Two pieces of net or old net curtain – the surface texture will play a role in the surface texture of your silk paper
- Silk tops, throwster's waste (dyed or undyed) or try other fibres
- Interesting bits and pieces of thread, fabric, petals, leaves and so on.
- Made-up wallpaper paste (buy a cheap one without additives)

### Technique
1. Place the plastic sheet on your working surface and put one piece of net on top.
2. Pull out your fibres into long pieces and place them, overlapping, on top.
3. Cut fibres of different colours, bits of thread or fabric, feathers, petals and leaves can all be incorporated at this stage.
4. Place a fine layer of silk fibres on top of any incorporated bits.
5. Place the second piece of net on top of the fibres.
6. Work the wallpaper paste into the fibres through the net.
7. Turn over the work carefully (with the fibre strands sandwiched between two pieces of net) and place them the other way up on the plastic surface. Now work the paste into this side as well until there are no more dry patches.
8. Hang the paper up to dry. I find it useful to pull away one side of the net surface before the paper is totally dry.
9. Once dry, pull the remaining net gently away from the paper surface. You can speed up the drying process with a hairdryer.

*Right: Silk paper with incorporated petals.*

*Below: Silk paper with incorporated feathers and fish scales. The feathers were collected in an orchard, the iridescent scales are from a carp, carefully dried and disinfected.*

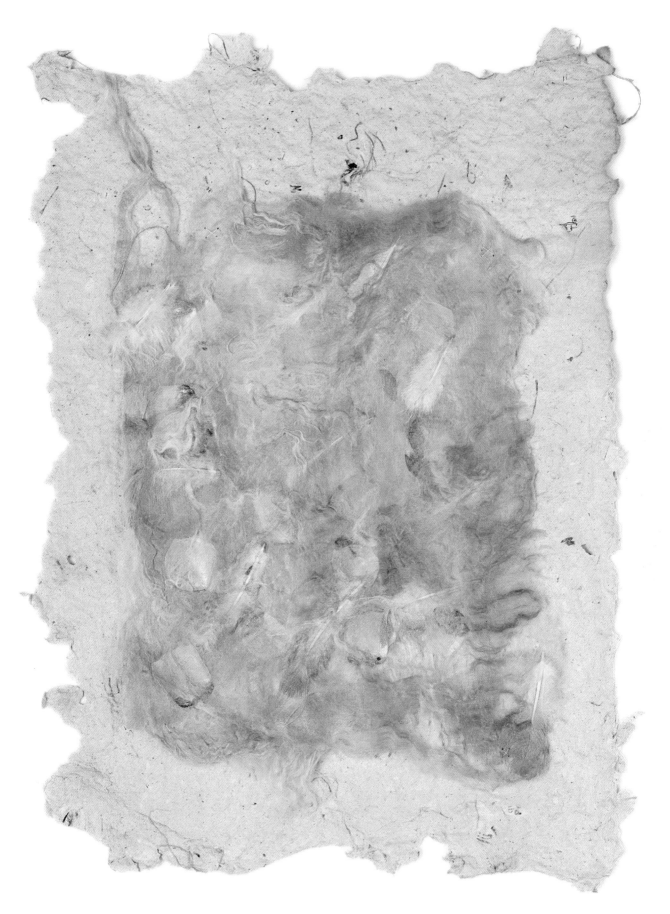

**PROJECT: SILK PAPER BOWL**

It is easy to make beautiful three-dimensional objects with silk paper

1.  Follow stages 1–4 on page 12.
2.  Place a piece of plastic kitchen film on top of the paper.
3.  Mould the paper over a bowl or mould (a balloon can be particularly useful).
4.  The net can be gently pulled away for easier moulding and drying.
5.  When the paper is dry, gently pull it off the bowl or mould, or pierce the balloon so that it deflates slowly.
6.  Gently pull away the kitchen film.

These papers are strong enough to be hand or machine stitched although, if your stitching is to be heavy, you will have to treat them very gently or place them on a surface that will give them support.

HARDENING THE SURFACE OR WATERPROOFING

The paper surface can be made harder by painting on successive coats of PVA medium, but for a rock-hard and watertight result try Paverpol. This is a textile hardener, perfectly safe to use, which hardens textiles, leather, paper, flowers and so on. It sticks to everything except plastic. The result can be used outdoors, but not in humid conditions unless the item has been treated with the special varnish available in matt or satin finish. Alternatively, you can add Paverplast to create pieces that remain completely watertight. This does make the Paverpol a little stiffer and, if it is too stiff to paint on your very delicate silk paper, you may choose the option of varnish instead.

You can choose to harden your silk paper shape once it is made, formed and stitched. The advised way of using Paverpol is by dipping fabric into it, but you can paint it onto a surface too.

**You will need:**
*   Paverplast powder
*   A pot of Paverpol translucent
*   Varnish in matt or shiny or Paverplast if you want your form to be watertight

**Technique**
1.  Mix the Paverplast powder into the liquid Paverpol if you want to make the object waterproof. Use 100 g (3½ oz) per 1 litre (35¼ fl oz).
2.  Paint the liquid hardener onto one side of the form. This can be done by carefully holding it in your hand. The liquid will start to soften your paper, so sooner or later you will need to put it over a mould to form the work or help it to hold its shape. It's better to put the form over something rather than in it as, in its wet state, the paper could lose its shape. Apply thinly, working the hardener into the surface with a medium brush (not too hard or soft). If the hardener is applied too thickly, it can flake or crackle if manipulated before being totally dry.

3. Once it is dry you can paint the other side without difficulty.

4. If you found the Paverplast unsuitable and wish to render the object watertight, you can do so once the Paverpol is completely dry and hard. (It's best to allow a week.)

5. Now you can pass a coat of varnish over the inside and outside of the bowl or form. Both matt and silk finish varnish are available. You will still have the look of a delicate textile, with the colours and stitching that you have included in the work, undamaged by the hardening process.

## CHEAT'S SILK PAPER

Traditional methods of making silk paper can be bypassed by using dissolvable fabric, particularly Aquabond, if your aim is to machine embroider on the final surface.

1. Spread silk tops onto Aquabond to cover the surface lightly or more heavily. One way of making this easy and less sticky is to take off the backing fabric only in the area you want to use. To do this, score through the backing paper and pull off the central part that you need. The paper edging may even help you to use your fabric surface without a hoop if you prefer. If the work you wish to create is smaller than the hoop you can score around the inside of the hoop and just pull off the backing on the inside – this prevents your hoop from getting sticky.

2. Machine stitch onto the surface – several lines of light stitching will suffice, but you can embroider as much or as little as you like. The advantage of creating your paper on a vanishing fabric is that it gives you a strong support for any stitching, particularly if you wish to incorporate heavy areas of stitching.

3. Dissolve the vanishing fabric and pat dry with a towel or kitchen towel.

4. Place the work on the backing paper that you took off the Aquabond, or on baking parchment – it's important that the work dries on a non-stick surface.

Your paper is finished – it is relatively fragile, but can be beautifully delicate and transparent.

*Right: Finished silk bowl, made firmer with Paverpol.*

# WORKING WITH WOOL AND OTHER ANIMAL FIBRES

Wool fibres have tiny overlapping scales, which allow them to be felted together to create a firm fabric through the use of moisture, friction and, possibly, heat. When the fibres are rubbed together in a wet environment, these scales lock together. The more they are rubbed, the more they will lock and the stronger the felt will be. Throughout history this process has been employed differently in many parts of the world to convert wool into a strong fabric. There is therefore not only one way to make felt, but many ways of achieving it – each felt maker develops their own techniques.

Creating wool felt is a relatively easy but time-consuming process. Different wools have a different thickness, with finer or coarser scales. The thickness or fineness of felt that can be made is variable according to the wool fibres used. For the beginner the easiest fibres to use are wool tops.

## FELT

**You will need:**

- Old towels – folded onto a table so that they don't hang over the sides
- Bubble wrap or fine plastic wrapping
- Wool tops – merino are a good choice for the beginner, either dyed or undyed
- Any bits and pieces of thread or fabric for inclusion
- Warm soapy water (made from real soap flakes)
- A pole, dowel or a bamboo mat

## Technique

1. Place one layer of bubble wrap onto the towels.
2. Put a layer of net on top.
3. Pull the fibres and spread them out, laying them in one direction.
4. Place another layer of fibres at right angles to the first layer.
5. A third layer can be placed over the second layer in the same direction as the first layer, or you can lay this last layer of fibres in different directions to create movement. You can also incorporate other bits and pieces and fibres into this last layer.
6. Place the second layer of net on top and rub the warm or hot soapy water into the work until it is completely wet.
7. Place the dowel at one end of the work and roll it up.
8. You now have to create a friction by rolling and unrolling the work. One way of doing this is to place the work vertically over a bowl and roll the dowel between your hands, making sure that the roll doesn't come undone – a few tacking stitches along the end will ensure this if necessary. Do this several hundred times. Also, hotter water can be added if the felting process is inconclusive; you can tell this by looking at the edges to see if the layers of fibres separate.

*Right:* Murano. *Different coloured silk tops were stuck to Aquabond and stitched. The original sketchbook drawing was in watercolours. Once dissolved, the embroidered pieces were laid flat on an artists' canvas painted with acrylic paint and bronze powders.*

Alternatively, roll the felt backwards and forwards, rolled up in a bamboo mat. Count a hundred times at least.

There are no secrets to felt making: the process of causing the fibres to felt is physical and can take time.

## CHEAT'S FELT 1

This process can produce a very fine 'wool paper' or 'felt', much finer than is usually possible with the normal felting process. The result can be stitched into, although placing it on a firmer backing is recommended. (This could be a vanishing fabric.)

1. Place the plastic sheet on your working surface and put one piece of net on top.
2. Pull out your merino fibres as long as possible and place them, overlapping, on top.
3. Cut fibres of different colours; bits of thread or fabric, petals and leaves or silk tops can all be incorporated at this stage.
4. Place a fine layer of merino fibres on top of any incorporated bits. If you don't incorporate any bits and pieces, you may use one layer of very fine wool tops.
5. Place a second piece of net on top of the fibres.
6. Work cellulose wallpaper paste into the fibres through the net.
7. Turn over the work carefully (with the fibre sandwiched between the two pieces of net) and place them the other way up on the plastic surface. Now work the paste into this side until there are no more dry patches.
8. Hang the paper up to dry thoroughly.
9. Once it is dry, pull the net gently away from the paper surface.

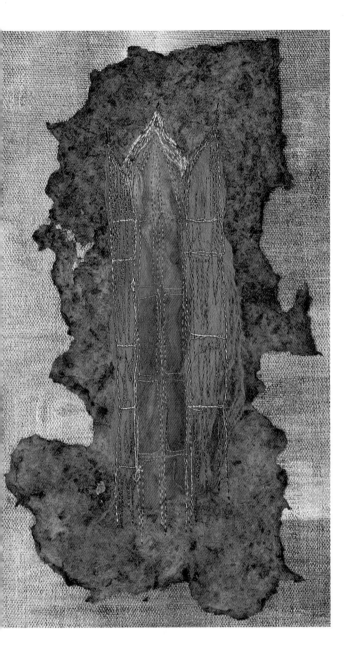

## CHEAT'S FELT 2

The interesting aspect of creating a 'felt' in this way is that you can create a surface out of wool that is really delicate and fine, particularly with merino wool tops as you need only use one layer of fine wool fibres, unlike felt. Merino wool tops are available dyed in many colours if you do not wish to dye your own. You can incorporate any objects into the surface, just as with real felt.

1.  Spread wool tops onto Aquabond to cover the surface lightly or more heavily as desired.
2.  Machine embroider on the surface – several lines of light stitching will suffice, but you can embroider as much or as little as you like. The advantage of creating your wool 'felt' on a vanishing fabric is that it gives you a strong support for any stitching, particularly if you wish to incorporate heavy areas of embroidery. You may also incorporate objects such as feathers, petals, leaves, or silk tops and other fibres into the surface of the felt.
3.  Dissolve the vanishing fabric and pat dry with a towel or kitchen towel.
4.  Place the work on the backing paper that you took off the Aquabond, or on baking parchment – it's important that the work dries on a non-stick surface. Your 'felt' is finished!

*Above:* Venetian Window with Blue Shutters. *The window is worked on silk 'paper' and the shutters are of Cheat's Felt I. The paper and felt were made together and are incorporated together. They are stitched onto handmade paper made with autumn leaves (see page 65) and presented on a painted artists' canvas.*

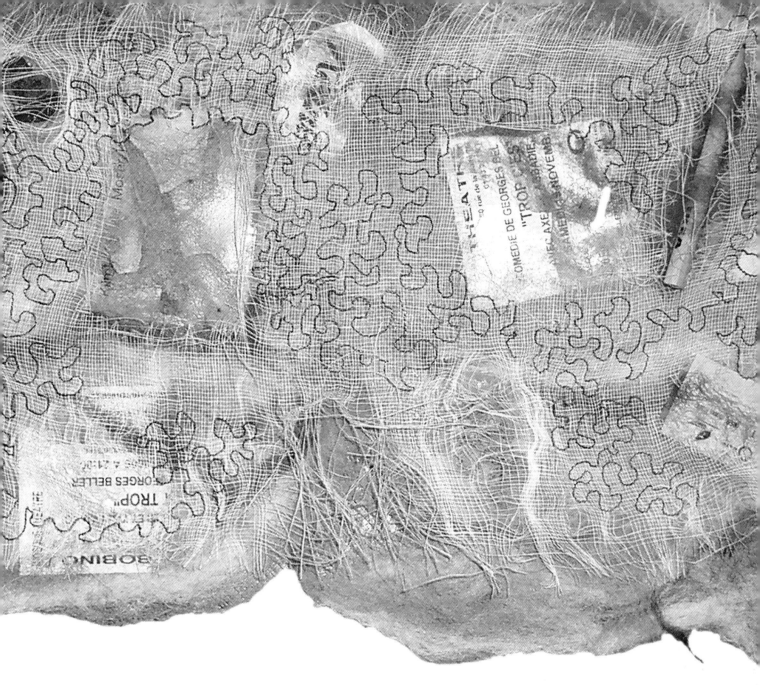

## FOUND ANIMAL HAIR

Wool found on fences or combed out pet or horse hair can all be combined in the any of the previous processes or used to create 'cheat's felt'. Washing is important, so follow the guidelines below.

### Technique

1. Wash in hot soapy water by plunging the fibres into the water and taking them out, and repeating the process until the visible dirt is lifted. If necessary. put the fibres in a net bag – the open type that you buy vegetables in is ideal or stocking bags for the washing machine.
3. Wash out the suds in clear warm water.
4. Wash out again in clear cold water – with luck the smell of the fibres will have been lifted too.

*Above:* Paris *by Martine Gatefin. Wool and silk fibres, cat hair, muslin and objects from a trip to Paris are incorporated into this piece.*

# WORKING WITH COTTON AND LINEN

Cotton fibres are a traditional source of papermaking, but both cotton and linen fibres can be used. To reduce the fibres from old rags to fibres suitable for papermaking, paper mills use special machines, although, before these were invented, cotton rag was simply torn or cut into very small pieces and beaten with a series of hammers. Producing such fibres in the home without the specialist equipment would be ridiculously time consuming – the liquidiser that is so useful in papermaking won't cope with it. However, small pieces of fabric can be incorporated into recycled papermaking or into the following process. Cotton tops, rag fibres, linen tops or spinner's waste can be used to create a 'paper' in the same way as silk fibres. For paper recycling see pages 54–67.

## COTTON OR LINEN 'PAPER'

### You will need:

- A plastic sheet or cling film (san wrap)
- Two pieces of net or old net curtain – the surface texture will play a role in the surface texture of your silk paper
- Cotton tops, cotton rag fibres, linen tops or spinner's waste, leftover threads, studio floor sweeping, and so on.
- Interesting bits and pieces of thread, fabric, petals, leaves, feathers, bark etc.
- Made-up wallpaper paste (buy a cheap one without additives)

### Technique

1. Place the plastic sheet on your working surface and lay a piece of net on top.
2. Pull out your fibres as long as possible and place them, overlapping, on top.
3. Cut fibres of different colours – bits of thread or fabric, feathers, petals and leaves can all be incorporated at this stage.
4. Place a fine layer of fibres on top of any incorporated bits. You can arrange colours and textures quite carefully if you wish.

*Below left: Cotton 'felt' made with children's glitter. The cotton came directly from a cotton flower in seed, which was part of a Christmas bouquet.*

*Below centre: Linen 'paper' with autumn leaves incorporated.*

*Below right: Linen 'paper' painted with gold bronzing powders in acrylic wax.*

5. Place the second piece of net on top of the fibres.
6. Work the wallpaper paste into the fibres through the net.
7. Turn over the work carefully (with the fibres sandwiched between the two pieces of net) and place them the other way up on the plastic surface. Now work the paste into this side as well until there are no more dry patches.
8. Hang the paper up to dry – I find it useful to pull away one side of the net surface before the paper is totally dry.
9. Once it is dry, pull the remaining net gently away from the paper surface. You can speed up the drying process with a hairdryer.
10. Experiment with the fibres to create fine or heavyweight surfaces.

*Above: Cotton 'paper' made with cotton tops and incorporated feathers.*

## SOFT COTTON TOP 'FELT'

This method of creating a soft fused surface can be adapted to wool and silk tops too. The size of the piece of fabric to be created shouldn't exceed the length of the tops as it will not hold together in the way that felt or 'paper' will.

1. On a piece of baking parchment place a layer of cotton tops, teased out.
2. Sprinkle with bonding glue – the amount required will come with practice. You need more than you would put on if you were adding salt to your dish – perhaps as much as sugar on strawberries?
3. Place another layer of cotton tops at right angles to the first and sprinkle again with bonding glue as before.
4. Follow with another layer of cotton tops in the same direction as the first layer.
5. Cover with another layer of baking parchment and iron to melt the glue.
6. When the work has cooled slightly, you can remove the paper. If you have not included enough glue, the layers will separate easily and you can try again.
7. Include anything you like with the layers – bits of thread and fabric, leaves, and so on.
8. The surface is suitable for hand or machine stitching.

# WORKING WITH SYNTHETIC FUSIBLE FIBRES

Many synthetic fibres in nylon, polyester or other derivatives will fuse together with heat and pressure. You can test this by ironing the fibres while they are sandwiched between baking parchment, so that the fibres don't stick to the hot iron or the ironing surface.

Fibres, such as Angelina fibres and Crystal Strands, can be bought for fusion. The sparkly fibres available for Christmas decorations often have properties of fusion under heat too, or can be included with Angelina or Crystal Strands fibres, so you can recycle your Christmas decorations into glitzy embroidery surfaces. To test any fibres to see if they will fuse proceed as follows:

**Precaution:** You should wear a mask and work in a well-ventilated room. Stop if you feel uncomfortable. The fibres could catch fire, so work with a large bowl of water nearby just in case.

*Below: Fusible fibres – Crystal strands and Christmas decorations, with nylon scrolled thread form waves. (the scrolled thread came from in between bathroom tiles to protect them during storage). The stitching is free machine embroidery with weaver's rayon thread in the needle, using a reduced top tension and a top stitch needle.*

### Technique

1. Lay a piece of baking parchment on an ironing board. Lay the fibres out on the baking parchment so that they overlap densely or more sparsely as desired.
2. Place another piece of baking parchment over the fibres and iron with an iron set on the silk setting. Move the iron over the surface of the paper and don't allow the iron to stay too long in one place. The fibres should bond together fairly quickly, so check from time to time to see how things are going. The cooler iron setting will help the fibres to keep their iridescence and softness, but if the fibres haven't fused, gradually increase the temperature of the iron.

3. If you used a dense amount of fibres, and they are bonded from one side but not the other, turn the work over and iron from the other side.

4. If you are using a hot temperature with the iron in place for a long time and the fibres still haven't fused, then the fibres that you have found are not suitable for this technique. However, these fibres could be included in small quantities with others that are suitable.

- When buying fusible fibres, you will have noticed that certain products do not fuse well and these have to be incorporated with the fusible fibres.
- Note that any edges that you cut away can be re-incorporated into future projects – you don't need to throw them away!

You can make anything from fine gossamer lacy fabrics to dense stiff surfaces using these fibres. You can mix different colours and different fibres (Angelina, Crystal Strands or old Christmas decoration fibres) for different effects. Other materials might include:

- Small quantities of wool, silk or other natural fibres or cast-off hand or machine embroidery threads placed between layers of fusible fibres.
- Small pieces of fabric or cut-out shapes.
- Sequins and other decorative paper or metallic shapes.

*Above:* The World is your Oyster *(detail). Centre of the piece, with shell incorporated and beads added (see page 96 for the whole piece).*

- Feathers, petals or leaves. (If the areas to be incorporated are too large to allow the fusible fibres to stick together, you could use small bits of Bondaweb or bonding glue.)
- Wire, which can be used later on to form the fusible fibre fabric into sculptural shapes. (It is best to use fine wires and curl or bend them so that they don't pull out too easily.)

*Below: A fusible fibre bowl, made from Christmas decoration fibre, with a small mount of Angelina on the inside. The edge of the bowl was burned with a soldering iron.*

## MAKING HOLES

Having created your fibre you can burn it using your favourite method – joss stick, hot wire or fine soldering iron.

You can pin or tape your fibre to a frame if you are using a wire or joss stick, or place it on a wooden board if you are using a soldering iron. Your design can be burned into the surface of the fusible fibres just as with other polyester and synthetic fibres.

**MOULDING**

Fusible fibres can easily be moulded over textured surfaces or into formed shapes while hot. The result will be permanent, although if you do not like the result, you can reheat it and try again. It's easiest to make your fabric first by following the method used for testing the fibres.

- **Shaping the fusible fibre:** While the fibre is still hot, you can take it out from between the baking parchment and roll it into a cone or tube. You can stick together the join on the tube or cone by reheating it between the parchment.
- **Moulding for texture:** Place the fusible fibre fabric, still in its baking-parchment sandwich, over the textured object or mould, and reheat until the fabric has taken on the texture. You can use printing blocks or other heat-resistant objects with clear texture. If you don't like the result, you can always reheat and start again.
- **Moulding for shape:** Cover a bowl with a carefully folded layer of silicone paper. Place the fibres over this, or use a ready-made sheet of fibres. Place another sheet of silicone paper over this and iron carefully around the bowl. The use of a metal bowl will help to transfer the heat. If the inside isn't stuck as it should be, place the fibre bowl on the inside of the bowl mould and iron carefully with the silicone paper in place.

- You can colour the results with wax crayons or metallic wax crayons, transfer paints (which are made for synthetic fibres), acrylic paints, bronzing powders in acrylic wax, transfer foils, relief paints, and so on.
- All the surfaces are suitable for hand or machine stitching. You may try to include any lightweight stitching into the fusible fibre surface before it is to be moulded into a form, as it may be more difficult to stitch it afterwards. This will only work if the stitching isn't too heavy for the fibres to melt and reform.

# APPLIQUÉ

All the surfaces dealt with in this chapter can be applied to other surfaces for stitching if desired (from the point of view of richness of design), or if necessary (if the surface or fabric created is too fragile to be stitched or presented on its own).

All natural fibre constructions can be cut to a shape or left as they are; synthetic fibre can be cut with scissors or a soldering iron.

To apply them to a surface you can simply use stitching, bonding glues (in powder or web form) or PVA medium. Too much PVA or bonding webbing may detract from or over-flatten the fibres applied, so do be careful.

# CHAPTER TWO
# RECYCLING FABRIC WASTE

Throughout history there are examples or using unworn second-hand fabrics or parts of old embroideries to create slips or bands for new garments or household items. Threads or beads were even unpicked and reused for economy. The use of the good parts of old worn fabrics for patchwork is obviously part of a cultural heritage where need and scarcity dictated a make-do-and-mend mentality. War years created a need for reuse through the scarcity of available new materials, and many people approached these constraints in a creative way.

The development of creative reuse of fabrics owes its starting point to these years of need and scarcity, but using the worn or good parts of pre-used textiles can also make a statement. Many of today's creators are influenced by their memories of this frugality, which they experienced throughout the war and during rationing, combined with a reaction against the fashion in embroidery towards expensive materials and costly components. Clearly the recycling of fabrics makes an economic statement about consumerism and society's readiness to create unnecessary waste; but the former use of the objects incorporated into a piece can also become part of its statement – attaching the former history of the fabric concerned to the new textile that has been created. Recycling old fabrics into new surfaces can thus create rich and rewarding results. The old fabrics come back to a new life, but bring with them their own past and stories.

## RECYCLING FABRICS INTO PATCHWORK

Stitching and re-inventing patchwork, appliqué or crazy patchwork using old fabrics can be creative, but needs to be approached with care if the result is not to be an uncontrolled mishmash of colour and uncoordinated shape. The control necessary could be achieved by:

- Using fabrics of just one colour or choosing a harmonious colour scheme. (You could perhaps dye all the fabrics in the same dye bath so that, in spite of their intrinsic colour or pattern, they have a harmony of their own.)
- Using fabrics that are similar in texture, or of the same origin, within a controlled colour scheme.

If you are using a collection of fabrics without an intrinsic homogeneity, try to create control with the structure of the work (using the same shapes, or even the same size shapes), or a style of patchwork that in itself is relatively controlled (strip patchwork or log cabin, for example).

The fabrics could be given a homogeneity after being patched by dyeing the work in a dye bath – do this carefully so that all the fabrics take on the same amount of dye and it is just their patterns or the starting colour that show through, which will make all the difference. Alternatively, put the work in a dye bath that is insufficient and add water to the dye bath. Some areas will receive less dye than others and the result will be patchy.

You could use tie dyeing instead to give a different effect, and the patchwork pieces that are different colours or patterns will show through where the dye was unable to take. You will need to use a strong dark colour for this to be effective.

A different reuniting factor for the patchwork could be the origin of the fabrics or surfaces included, which could offer a visual harmony as well as a conceptual one: a patchwork made of paper where the pieces come from one book; a patchwork made of cast-off carrier bags; a patchwork made from one garment cut up and re-stitched, and so on.

Crazy patchwork was a quick and easy way of stitching any shape of fabric together using decorative but functional hand stitching that was relatively quick to do. It allowed for good bits of fabric to be cut out of worn-out clothes and household items. Any shapes could be cut, and these could be assembled in a haphazard fashion that avoided waste. Many of the original hand stitches – feather stitch, cretan stitch and fly stitch – now find themselves copied in machine programs to produce look-alike crazy patchwork. Machine stitching can be used to stitch over the edges instead of the decorative hand stitching, allowing for a surface that holds together more firmly. You can do this traditionally by stitching the pieces together over each other or against each other without a foundation or backing fabric, or include a foundation fabric for ease of stitching and manipulation. Without a foundation fabric all the pieces included in the crazy patchwork need to be of more or less the same weight. If you use a foundation fabric, you will be able to juggle with different weights of fabric as well as different colours, sizes and shapes.

There are many books available with different patchwork patterns and techniques, so I will just concentrate on a few of the more unusual techniques.

*Above:* Il Était une Fois une Tapis (Once Upon a Time There Was a Carpet) *by Mireille Vallet; Silk noile, silk and cotton dyed in madder, procion-dyed cotton, red printed cotton and linen. The thread in the needle was an invisible thread and the bobbin threads were rayon and madder-dyed silk, which used the different nuances from where the silk hank was attached. The prints were reproduced from Persian carpets and old cashmere fabrics and transferred with a transfer fabric paper (Lazertran). The fabrics were torn and placed between two layers of soluble fabric, and the stitching was worked from one piece of fabric to the other so that the bobbin thread would be seen.*

## SEAMED OR STRIP PATCHWORK

Seaming old bits and pieces of fabric together in a haphazard way was the busy woman's patchwork. A way of make-do-and-mend that could be quickly achieved by hand, or very often, by machine. This avoided cutting out complicated shapes and the reliance on many different designs and colour schemes that perhaps the available fabrics couldn't supply. Laborious decorative hand stitching with expensive threads could also be bypassed.

Seminole patchwork is a decorative patchwork achieved by seaming fabrics together in strips, and then cutting those strips and reassembling them to produce a pattern. Again, books abound on this technique that was exploited with the advent of the sewing machine. However, seaming or stitching together in strips, cutting up the result and then re-stitching it together can produce complicated and decorative surfaces, either alone or as a starting point for further embroidery and stitching.

Any old fabrics can be used for this, dyed or left as you find them. You could incorporate sweet wrappers, plastic bags, or any other found objects, and work by hand or machine.

### Technique

1. Cut your chosen pieces into strips – the length will depend on what length you can cut within the fabric or wrapper you are using, but the longer the better, if you wish to make a sizeable piece. A lot of fabric is lost in the seams. The strips can be cut in any width – allow for seaming, but fine widths can be very decorative. Avoid making the strips too wide or the result may be quite clumsy.
2. Seam the fabrics together following one of the following methods:
   - Put them face to face and stitch the narrowest seam possible that will hold on the chosen fabric. Open out the pieces and iron flat. (This is the traditional method).
   - Place them side by side and chose a zigzag or decorative stitch that will stitch from one of the strips into its neighbour.
   - Place one slightly over its neighbour and stitch them together with a straight stitch, zigzag or decorative stitch.

*Right top: Strips of fabric stitched alternately with sweet wrappers using a zigzag stitch.*

*Right bottom: The materials have been cut into strips at right angles, and stitched back together with a machine zigzag.*

3. Cut the finished piece into strips at right angles to the previous seams. Move the pieces around until you have achieved the desired effect and stitch them together using one of the above methods. Alternatively:
   - Instead of cutting at right angles, as in step 3, experiment with 45-degree angles and other ways of cutting into the strips. When positioning the fabrics together again, you will achieve diamonds or triangles.
   - The work can be further embellished with decoration such as cords, beads, further stitching and so on.

## SCULPTURE IN PATCHWORK

Using strips of fabric dipped in Paverpol can be a different way of creating patchwork sculpture.

Paverpol is a textile hardener, perfectly safe to use, which hardens textiles, leather, paper, flowers and so on. It sticks to everything except plastic. The result can be used outdoors, but best not in humid conditions unless it is treated with the special varnish available in matt or satin finish. You can add Paverplast to the Paverpol to create pieces that remain completely watertight. Use 100g (3½ oz) per 1 litre (35¼ fl oz).

### You will need:

- Fabric
- Scissors
- A frame or armature to support your fabric
- Paverplast or varnish if you want the result to be watertight
- Paverpol translucent (available in pots)

### Technique

1. Cut up strips or shapes of your chosen fabrics. Do this in advance because, once you start the process, things become messy. Consider what you are trying to achieve. You could be making strip patchwork, shell shapes, diamonds, squares or round shapes. Bear in mind that they will have to completely overlap on your framework if you are trying to make something watertight; you can leave spaces if this is not an issue. You could embroider the fabric beforehand for added texture and then cut it up into shapes.

2. Make an armature or form out of metal wire, wire form, a balloon, wood (the product will stick and the wood will become part of it) or anything else that seems appropriate. If you wish to be able to withdraw the armature once dry, check that it doesn't stick to the fabric hardener. For long slim pieces, I use an armature of coiled plastic-coated electrical wire, leaving a piece out to pull on – this could even be suspended for ease of construction and drying. Once dry (not rock hard) I can easily pull the wire out as it uncoils. If you wish the result to be watertight use Paverplast mixed in with the Paverpol in the proportion of 100 g (3½ oz) to 1 litre (35¼ fl oz).

3. Dip the pieces of fabric into the fabric hardener, one by one. As you pull it out, wring it out between two fingers by pulling it through your fingers like an old fashioned laundry wringer. This is essential: if the fabric is too wet, it becomes difficult to handle and sculpt.

4. Layer the pieces on the armature, covering with one layer and ensuring there aren't any gaps. Place as many layers as you wish, but one is quite sufficient.

5. Allow the work to dry – it can take up to a week to become thoroughly hard. Remove the armature at this stage if it is your intention to do so.

6. Once it is dry, you can colour or varnish the result if you wish, or allow your patchwork pieces to speak for themselves.

Left: Strips of an old summer suit were dipped in fabric hardener and wrapped around a wire coil structure which was removed once dry. A cord was made by stitching together a collection of leftover knitting cottons and wools with a wide zigzag. This was attached and painted with fabric hardener.

## PATCHWORK ONTO VANISHING FABRIC

Creating patchwork with vanishing fabric as a foundation or backing can literally open up the possibilities of patchwork. Although you can create patchwork by trapping the pieces of fabric that you want to patch together between two layers of Aquafilm dissolvable, using Aquabond can make the process even easier.

### Technique

1.  Peel off the backing of the Aquabond and stick the prepared cut out fabrics onto the surface as desired. One way of making this easier and less sticky is to take off the backing fabric in the area you want to use. To do this score through the backing paper and pull off the central part that you need. The paper edging may even help you to use your fabric surface without a hoop if you prefer. If the work you wish to create is smaller than the hoop, you can score around the inside of the hoop and just pull off the backing on the inside.

2.  Stitch over the patches in such a way that they will be held together by the machine stitches or, depending on the design, you may be able to use hand embroidery as well, or instead of, machine stitching. Consider this stitching carefully. It's easy to stitch very heavily and be sure that everything will hold together. But by looking at the work carefully it is possible to see just how little stitching can be placed, how and where, so that the work is as light and airy as possible. Consider what you are trying to achieve visually with the stitching, as well as the technical requirement of holding the work together.

    If you are working with crazy patchwork, scattering the pieces onto Aquafilm or Solusheet may be sufficient instead of careful placement on Aquabond, as the exact position of the pieces will be less important.

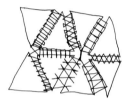

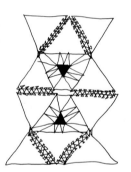

*Above: Pieces can be left out of the design to create holes, or the gaps can be filled with lacy stitching.*

*Right: Sample of stitching over edges to hold strips together on vanishing fabric*

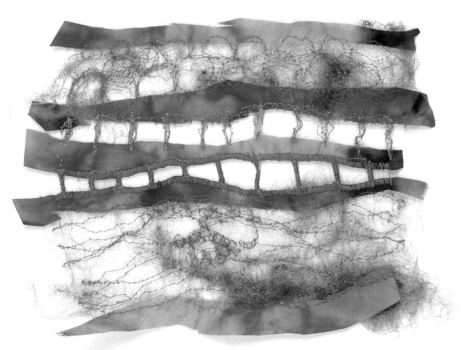

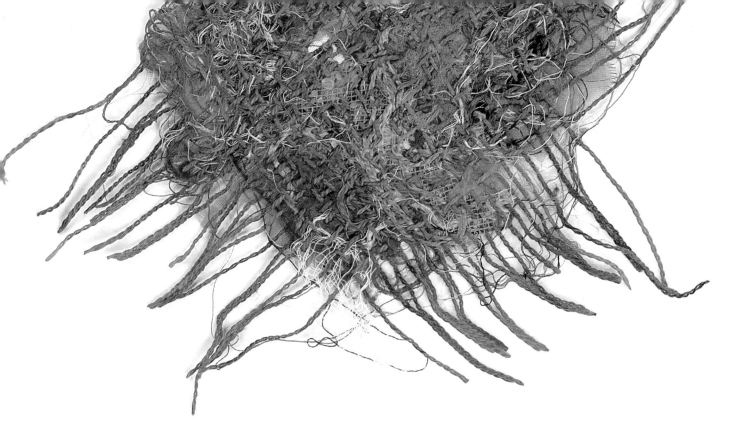

3. Once all the fabrics are held one to another, you can dissolve the backing fabric. Soak it for a few minutes or wash it under a running tap. Warm or hot water will make the Aquabond disappear best. The result can be a little hard as some residue will be left in the threads and fabrics at this stage. To fully dissolve this residue leave the work in a good quantity of water (in proportion to the size of the work) overnight.

**Ideas**

- Use traditional patchwork designs as a base for the work.
- The patchwork pieces can be cut out and placed next to each other on the dissolvable fabric and the edges stitched together.
- The pieces can be placed next to each other with a small gap left between them, which can be bridged by stitching.
- Pieces can be left out of the design to create holes or these can be filled with lacy stitching.
- Look at shape, contrasting shapes, repeated shapes and motifs, that might not be possible in traditional patchwork.
- The pieces can be placed as haphazardly and densely as a crazy patchwork and stitched over with running stitches, vermicelli, drunken wiggle or hand stitching.
- The pieces can be placed as a crazy patchwork but allow for holes or gaps to appear – the stitching will have to be considered carefully so that the work holds together.
- Inspiration can be found in subjects other than patchwork – waves in the sea, traces on the sand, long grass in a breeze, leaves on a tree, patterns in wood and so on.
- Working with computer programs such as Paintshop Pro or Photoshop, you may find patterns and shapes that you can develop from ordinary beginnings in photographs or drawings of your own.

*Above: Sweepings from the studio floor and bits of fabric and thread were trapped between two layers of fine Aquafilm. The rows of running stitch were left unknotted and worked alternately in each direction. They form an almost woven structure and the vanishing fabric was then dissolved.*

*Above:* Sea and Sand *by Mireille Vallet. Strips of fabric worked on vanishing fabric.*

# APPLIQUÉ AND REVERSE APPLIQUÉ

Stitching old fabrics together as in patchwork, adding fabrics on top for appliqué or cutting away areas to reveal other fabrics beneath as in reverse appliqué can create complex and beautiful surfaces.

### Ideas
- The appliqué or reverse appliqué can be done neatly by hand or machine, with turned-in or satin-stitched edges.
- Chop up the appliqué or reverse appliqué and stitch it on haphazardly, or cut it out roughly and just stitch here and there to create a fabric that is in 'decomposition'.
- Try distressing the surfaces further by sandpapering, bleaching or singeing.
- You can further embellish the surfaces with embroidery once they are stitched together and cut as necessary.

*Right:* Rags to Riches. *Reverse appliqué pieces by Maria Walker. Maria is drawn to recycling materials through an upbringing that encouraged thrift and reuse, and also as a reaction against today's consumption-orientated, throwaway society where labels are everything. The technique for these pieces is reverse appliqué, allowing for detailed images using layer upon layer of fabric.*

*Far Right:* Pedro Vista. *by Maria Walker. 'A Mallorcan countryside villa was crammed with numerous artifacts that inspired me to sketch a pastiche of patterns and shapes, which later became a basis for this piece of work'.*

*Opposite:* Moroccan Interior II *by Maria Walker.*

# DYEING AND DISCHARGING TECHNIQUES TO REUSE OLD FABRICS

Even old printed fabrics can be given a new lease of life for textile and embroidery work if they are dyed, or subjected to discharge techniques first.

## DYEING

For the dyeing techniques below, use your favourite dyes, Procion MX or whatever you find available. Mix them and fix them as instructed on the pack.

### Ideas

*   Try using different fabrics, with different prints or colours. Consider carefully your choice of old fabrics and the colour of the dye you are going to add so that you don't simply end up with a pile of muddy brown fabrics. Make sure they will take the dye that you are going to use and are washed and clean. Place them all in the same dye bath. How they absorb colour may vary, but be aware that their existing colours and patterns will be seen through the dye colour. If these are used together for a piece of patchwork they will match together well, but each will be different.
*   Try dyeing them in an insufficient dye bath where some of the existing fabric will not take on the colour. Make up a dye bath of colour and place the fabrics in it. Using this method the fabrics will soak up the dye and there will still be some dry areas. Now add more water to the dye bath until the fabrics are submerged. The colours will bleed into the areas that are now wet, but not to the same extent as those areas that were able to take up the dye properly.
*   Tie dyeing techniques with a variety of similar-coloured or patterned fabrics can also be interesting.

## DISCHARGING

Discharging can be relatively simple, and can create interesting fabric surfaces for embroidery. The colours and results obtained are not always predictable, which is what can make this technique so attractive.

### SIMPLE BLEACHING

*Right: Detail of a patchwork Margery's Unfinished Cream Silk Blouse by Ann Marie Stewart. Experimental silk painting with sugar and granules on cut-up blouse pieces donated by a friend. Machine piecing and free-motion quilting using rayon and copper metallic threads.*

Bleach will work on many dyes on cotton and linen surfaces, but silk and wool can disintegrate or tear easily – an effect that you could perhaps exploit!

### You will need:

*   Rubber gloves, apron and eye protection
*   Well ventilated, well protected working area with plastic-covered floor and tables, or work outside
*   Bleach
*   Water
*   Foam or synthetic brushes

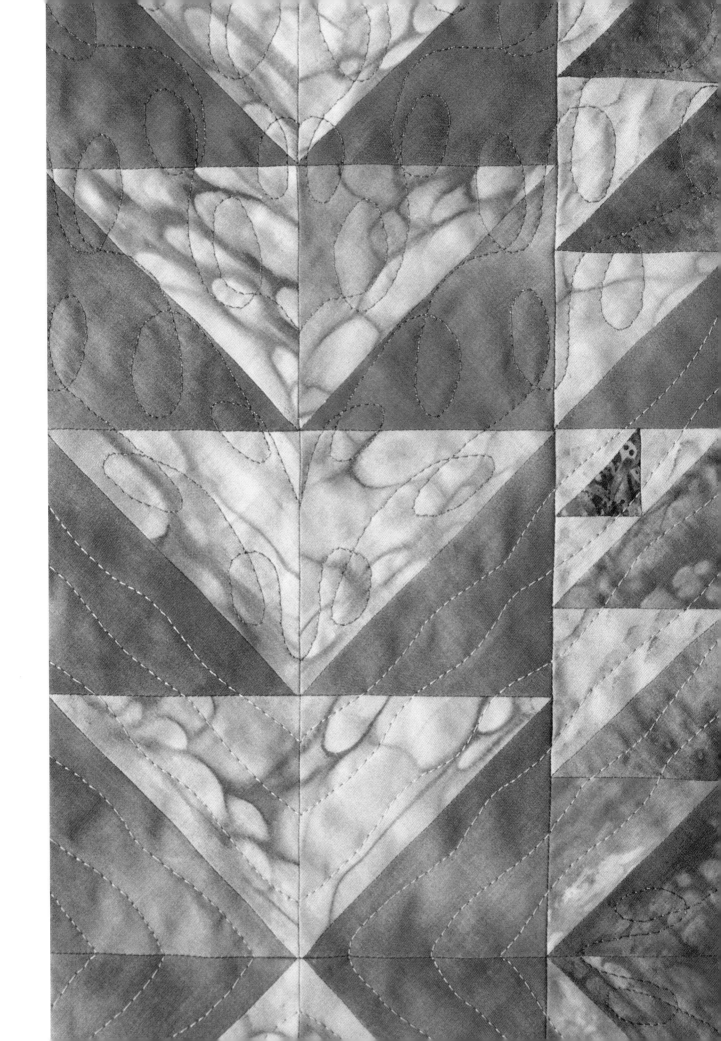

**Technique**

1.  Use bleach in dilutions of between five parts bleach to one part water or one part bleach to one part water. Do not exceed this ratio. You will need to test a small corner of the cloth with your diluted bleach mixture before embarking on a larger area.
2.  Liquid bleach can be spilled, painted on, or used in a dye bath with tie-dye methods. If painting, use foam or synthetic brushes as the bleach will cause natural ones to disintegrate.
3.  Once you have obtained the result you are looking for, you will need to stop the bleaching process. Do this by rinsing the work in lots of water, then putting it carefully in the washing machine and running it through a warm-wash cycle.

THICKENER

*Right: Shrug by Terri Jones. 'I have always loved fabrics and find it very difficult to throw anything away. My bedroom curtains were covered in dust and paint splashes from redecoration and faded from years of hanging in a sunny window when I reluctantly consigned them to the dustbin. Hours later – and in the pitch dark – I rescued them. Influenced by the rich textures and layering of the Tudor period the shrug has been constructed from off-cuts and leftovers, in unconscious imitation of the practice during the Tudor period of cutting up and reusing fabrics which were too precious to throw away when they became worn. The design was based on elaborate religious architecture seen on a journey through Brittany.'*

For a more precise use of bleach for discharge techniques you can mix the bleach with a thickener so that you can paint it on more carefully, or use print blocks, stencils, or cut sponges for clearer, more controlled, shapes.

To thicken the bleach mixture you will need to use Monagum thickener, which can also be used with reactive dyes. It is best to mix up a small quantity of Monagum paste and mix some of this with the bleach as and when you need it, as bleach will break down the Monagum thickener. The thickener can, however, be kept in a labelled jar in the refrigerator until needed if the bleach (or dye) has not been added.

**Technique**

1.  Sprinkle two tablespoons – around 9 g (⅓ fl oz) of monagum powder into 250 ml (8¾ fl oz) of warm water. Stir with a wire whisk, beater or blender, and allow to stand for a least 30 minutes or overnight. Remove lumps if necessary. Unused paste can be kept in the refrigerator for 6 months (label clearly) and unused powder will keep indefinitely at room temperature in dry conditions.
2.  Once your paste is ready, place the amount you wish to use in a plastic container and add the bleach a little at a time, mixing thoroughly to avoid lumps. Do not exceed the ratio of one part bleach to one part water. Test the reaction on the fabric you wish to use as you go. Note the reaction time.
3.  Neutralise the bleach as before or by soaking the fabric in a one part hydrogen peroxide to ten part water solution for ten minutes before washing the fabric in the washing machine. If the fabric falls apart after washing (too much bleach or weak fabric) make use of the bits and apply them to another fabric with embroidery.

**Ideas**

- Choose a fabric (preferably printed) that doesn't react to discharge dyeing. Dye the fabric with a strong-coloured dye that will react to your discharge paste. Use printing, painting or sponging to discharge the dye to reveal the work below.
- Discharge your fabric then paint or dye into the areas that have lost their colour.
- Use wood blocks, potato prints, plastic, crumpled plastic bags, sponges or other interesting surfaces to print motifs or designs with your discharge paste.
- Use the resulting fabric to influence your embroidery designs.

# WORKING INTO SECOND-HAND TEXTILE SURFACES

*Below right:* The Shirt Off Your Back *by Ann Wheeler. Shirts sourced from charity shops donated to start another life still bear original labels, fastenings and a lack of wear that emphasize our throwaway society.*

*Below: The 'wrong side' of the same piece.*

Old linen sheets or woollen blankets can offer interesting surfaces for new embroideries. Old linen sheets can be bought relatively cheaply second-hand, perhaps with a hole or two, and can be reused, cut and adapted as an economical surface for heavy embroidery. It can easily be dyed and, once the work is finished, it will stretch and hold its shape well. Woollen blankets can be felted (simply by washing them in a washing program that is too hot and not adapted for wool) and can thereafter be stitched and manipulated in the same way as ordinary felt. The felting process will reduce the size of your blanket, just as when you shrink a jumper, so be aware of this. Wool blankets can be dyed with most acid-based dyes. The resulting embroidery could take into consideration its origins – making a point of the stitching, holes, mends or decoration on the existing blanket or sheet. Alternatively, the blanket or sheet could simply be another useful surface like any other, as a support for your embroidery.

Cutting up an existing garment or undoing the seams can also be an interesting point of departure for new work. Pieces can be applied to new surfaces, presented as a patchwork, stitched on or reassembled. Their past will tell a story.

*Left:* Love is Fragile as Roses and Old Lace *by the author. Includes old laces, cotton tops, skeleton leaves, hydrangea petals and dried roses from a Valentine's day bouquet. These were stitched onto Solusheet before being dissolved.*

## LACE

Lace offers a superb surface for embroidery. Old laces have their own secret histories and meanings as well as bringing texture and pattern to a piece of work. The forms and patterns of the lace may prove inspirational for the stitching, or you can simply choose to ignore it and just allow the lace to provide a textural surface for further embroidery.

### WORKING WITH PAINT AND DYE ON LACE

Involving lace in painted and coloured surfaces will give a richness of texture to the work. Try the following to appreciate the different results you can achieve:

- Tear or chop up pieces of lace and place them on a surface. You can use pieces of adhesive webbing, PVA glue, rows of straight stitching, free machine embroidery following the lace design, or small discreet hand stitches to hold them into place.
- Try colouring with acrylic paint – use a paint that is supple such as Liquidex. If you wish to be able to embroider into the finished surface, add a little water to the paint so that it is not too thick. An additive for acrylic paint exists specially for painting on fabric surfaces that will make the surface more supple and easier to stitch on. The paint will give a homogeneous quality to the different laces, and the result will be an interesting textural surface for future work.
- Try dyeing the surface with fabric dyes, paints or transfers. In order to be able to do this you will need to have chosen laces that have more or less the same fibre content, or at least a fibre content that will be acceptable to your chosen dye. For example, you can mix cotton and linen lace and use dyes acceptable for cellulose dyes or paints and fixing methods. You may choose synthetics of various qualities and use transfer paints. The advantage here is that the different qualities of synthetics will take on the dye differently, and be more or less brilliant in colour, which may be interesting across the surface of the created fabric.
- Try using bronzing powders in acrylic wax over the laces to give a rich surface into which you can add more stitching and refinement.

### WORKING WITH LACE AND VANISHING FABRICS

The open quality of lace is lost in the above techniques, which concentrate solely on the textural quality of the lace. To exploit the open structure of lace, try using it in pieces on vanishing fabric, where you can allow the lace to hold areas of the structure together on its own. For the following experiments you will find the vanishing fabric Aquabond particularly useful, as you can stick the lace pieces to the surface of the vanishing fabric exactly where you want them to be, stitch, and then dissolve the fabric. If their exact position is less important you could work on Solusheet or between layers of Aquafilm.

- Chop up pieces of lace in a haphazard fashion and stick them to the surface of the vanishing fabric to create a crazy patchwork. Using traditional hand stitches such as herringbone or fly stitch, stitch these fabrics together so that, once the

*Above:* Empty Shrine *by the author. Glued and stitched-on lace coloured with acrylic paint and bronzing powders and treated with patina fluid.*

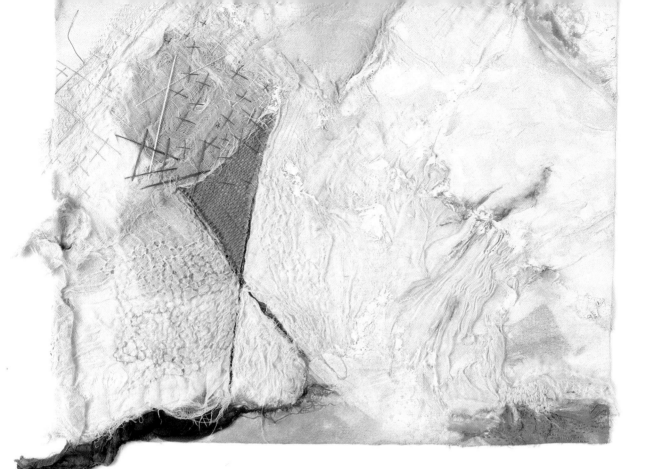

vanishing fabric has been dissolved, your lace patchwork will remain
stitched as one piece.

- Work as above but use the machine. Many modern sewing machines have an array of decorative stitches that resemble the traditional crazy patchwork stitches of fly and herringbone stitch; using your machine with a foot and the feed-dog up, you can stitch the crazy patchwork pieces together.
- Work as above but with free machine embroidery stitches, such as a drunken wiggle or stippling of fleece stitch, to hold the patchwork pieces firmly together.
- Now look at the patterns of the lace, and create a fabric that takes these patterns into consideration rather than just being 'crazy'. You may cut out different forms from the lace and place them on the surface of the vanishing fabric allowing gaps in between the laces so that they can each be appreciated instead of being a mishmash of textures. An all-over light fleece stitch or drunken wiggle could hold all this together, or you could carefully plan your stitching so that it adds to, and becomes part of, the lace design.
- The final surface of your remade lace could be dyed or coloured as above.
- You could try including other materials into the surface: skeleton leaves, flowers, petals or other organic materials, buttons, beads sequins or thread waste.

*Above:* Wall *by the author. Paint, lace, muslin and pulled work, hand and machine stitching.*

## WORKING WITH LACE ON HOT WATER VANISHING FABRIC

In order to dissolve hot water vanishing fabric completely it has to be placed in vigorously boiling water. One of the rather interesting qualities of hot water vanishing fabric is that, if it is not boiled but placed in a bath of water at 80°C it will scrunch up into a pleated surface and cause any work or fabric attached to it to do the

*Above:* Tea with Granny, *memories of crumpled old lace with tea for four (granny, mum and sister); hot water vanishing fabric with lace dyed in old tea, machine embroidery.*

*Below: Strips of muslin straight stitched onto hot water vanishing fabrics heated to 80°C.*

same. Interesting surfaces can be achieved by adding fabrics to hot water vanishing and following this process.

**Technique**

1.  Cut-up pieces of lace, net, muslin or a mixture of the above and stitch them onto the hot water vanishing fabric. The work will shrink according to the density of stitching and weight of fabric that you choose to use, so bear this in mind for your experiments and final piece. As an indication, the lace piece (shown left) shrank to about two-thirds of its original size. The butter muslin (shown below left), a more lightweight fabric, which is also more lightly stitched, shrank to a half its original size. You may stitch them on using the foot and feed-dog up on your machine using straight or wavy lines or decorative stitches, or use free-machine embroidery and embellish the lace designs. Holes may be left in the work as the hot water vanishing fabric will remain to hold the work together.

2.  In a saucepan of a suitable size, bring the water temperature up to 75–80°C. If you don't have a thermometer, small bubbles should begin to appear on the sides of the saucepan and, when one or two start to mount to the surface of the water, take the saucepan off the heat and plunge your embroidery into it. It will immediately shrink into a scrunched up, pleated surface. Alternatively, place the embroidered hot water vanishing fabric into warm water and gradually raise the temperature of the water until it starts to shrink. Stop the heat source immediately. The vanishing fabric will remain, but will be a little hard.

-   If the colour of the vanishing fabric is inappropriate to your work, a good way to colour it is to use good quality inks before you do the embroidery. Allow the ink to dry and proceed as above. The ink will remain stable during the heat process and the vanishing fabric will retain the colour.

-   The final result can be dyed or painted afterwards, and more embroidery and embellishment added.

-   Using butter muslin or other lightweight fabrics torn into strips can also give interesting surfaces using this method.

## STITCHING ONTO EXISTING GARMENTS TO CREATE NEW WEARABLES

Stitching on old garments can be a fashion statement, creating new interest in an old garment, or wearable art. Stitching on old garments can make a statement about the wearer or the nature of that particular garment: the garment may be wearable, but sculptural and installation works of this nature are very relevant to female and feminist art as we pose questions about the nature of the coverings we place on our bodies, and the reasoning behind the development of such objects.

Usually when we are stitching fabrics for garment making, the stitching is worked onto the fabrics first, before the fabrics are stitched together. This allows for shrinkage during stitching, or allows for the work to be stretched once it is stitched. If you are working on existing garments, this approach is more difficult.

### Ideas

- If perfection is important, the garment could be dismantled and then stitched. If necessary the pieces could be stretched using the seam allowance, or binding added to the seams so that you can stretch them.
- If you are prepared to accept some loss of shape, you can stitch directly onto the garment as it is made up.
- If areas to be stitched are relatively small you could back them with Stitch 'n Tear or similar stabilising fabric, and tear off the backing fabric around the embroidery once it is done.
- Instead of a backing fabric or paper you could use a dissolvable fabric, which will completely disappear once the stitching is finished. Aquabond is useful for this as it is sticky and will really help stabilize the fabric.
- Always work in a hoop to avoid pulling the fabric out of shape as much as possible, but never leave the hoop in place if you are not actually working within it, and move its position regularly to avoid leaving imprints in the fabric or embroidery.
- If your final aim is sculptural rather than wearable, you could consider sculpting your fabric by including wire in seams or elsewhere to create a structure, or using Paverpol as a fabric hardener to sculpt the garment once made.

*Below Left: Collagraphy on paper from parts of old jeans.*

*Below Right: Reverse side of old jeans collagraphy.*

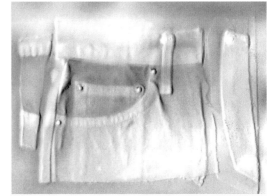

# CHAPTER THREE

# RECYCLING EMBROIDERY

For recycling embroideries, the most important starting point is really say to yourself: 'This work is only good for the dustbin, so it really doesn't matter what I do to it – I will learn something and things can only get better.' The second point is to completely ignore the origins of the embroidery. Why you did it, what it was meant to be, and, if it had a subject, ignoring that too. Remember you are not trying to turn around an unsatisfactory piece, adding a bit of something here and there to try and make the piece work – you've probably already been through that anyway, before deciding that it was only fit for the bin! This time you are starting on an already coloured and textured surface to make something completely new.

As you work, the piece may tell you how to treat it and what to add. It may also give you indications of what it is going to be – a band or decoration to be added to or become part of a garment, a piece of fabric that will be made into something suiting its size – perhaps a purse or bag, a pin cushion or cushion or a heavily stitched colourful panel. Allow the piece to gradually influence you as to its outcome and use. Perhaps you will finish by cutting up a heavily worked piece and turning it into greetings cards! You will hopefully have learned something about colour, texture and small-scale composition along the way.

## CUTTING UP AND PATCHING TOGETHER AGAIN

If the composition is too overpowering or there is a subject matter that is too present and real to be avoided, simply cutting the whole thing up into pieces to obliterate these constraints might be a good place to begin! Starting with these bits and pieces you could work on different types of backing.

### WHAT TO USE
- Vanishing fabrics – space the pieces out to leave holes or lacy nets.
- A plain cotton, linen or heavy silk – the cut-up bits or the stitching that joins them will entirely cover the surface.
- An already worked fabric – the base fabric is already dyed or coloured in an interesting way, painted or even partially stitched before receiving the cut-up bits and pieces.
- Inclusion into a surface – the bits and pieces of cut-up embroidery could be included into paper or cheat's paper (see page 54), silk paper (see page 15) or papier-mâché.

Now you can consider how to place the bits and pieces:

- Throw them in the air and see how they land (perhaps turn them the right way up) and glue them or bond them in place.
- Arrange them according to colour. You could use a patchwork or mosaic influence to help you to position the pieces.
- Change them in relation to your original composition, but be influenced by the same influences that inspired the original – perhaps you can keep the notion of 'landscape' or 'India' or whatever you already had – at least the colours will be appropriate.
- Look at the coloured pieces you have in front of you in a new light and see if the colours or textures that they offer can inspire something completely different to use as the source of influence.
- You could include the cut-up pieces with other pieces of fabric to enhance the colour scheme or add textural interest.

Once you have decided where to position the pieces on the chosen surface you can glue, bond, stitch, or temporarily pin them into place.

If you had chosen to include paper or fibre you may not need to add any stitching, but you may need to colour the surface so that everything becomes integrated.

*Right: A panel was worked on a Janome embroidery machine using Sfumato, which is a photo stitch program. The original photograph was of fishing nets and cages in a Brittany port, but as an embroidery worked on net it became a confused collection of coloured marks – attractive, but without any intrinsic sense. Turning it into a vase is one way to exploit its delicate qualities.*

## STITCHING AND ADDING

The following ideas can be added to your cut-up and re-pieced work, but you could also adapt them for use without cutting the original embroidery into pieces.

- Stitching by hand or machine, dyeing, painting, adding beads and so on can all help to integrate the pieces or obliterate the original intention of the work.
- Stitching can be worked over all of the surfaces, allowing the work underneath to peep through here and there. Try using machine zigzag stitch, or hand-running stitch.
- Stitching can just be about attaching the new pieces to the backing to allow the textures and colours present to really show.
- Stitching can be used to change the existing textures. Machine stitching into the larger textures of hand stitching can break it up and flatten it – leave some areas to stand proud. Hand stitching can add more textural interest to a machine-stitched surface.
- Adding beads, buttons, ribbons and cords or anything else that could disturb the original composition. Add beads in groups or buttons in ordered lines.
- Dye or paint all over the surface so that you are just using the textures of the original work and are integrating the whole work into a new uniformly coloured (or near uniform) piece.
- Using paint or oil pastels just lightly brushed over the surface might create an integrated surface without obliterating the work that has gone on before.
- Add another fabric over the surface of the work that will have some influence. This could be stitched over to integrate it into the surface.
- Fine nylon chiffon could integrate the surface.
- Dyed butter muslin pulled into holes by hand or with stitching could be stitched over the surface allowing the work beneath to show through.
- Synthetic organdie can be holed with heat tools.

## THE FINISHED OBJECT

Finally, you could simply readjust your ideas for the use of the piece. A panel could become a vase, or a bag, bits of a cushion, or be incorporated into a garment or household fabric. Liberating the embroidery from 'art to a 'craft object' for use could also liberate your mind set and increase your chances of success.

## PROJECT: CUSHION

Several bits and pieces and strips of embroidered fabric remained after I had made the make-up bag on page 50, so these were cut into even strips and applied with a drunken wiggle to a velvet backing. The backing was from an old torn dress that had been treated with discharge techniques.

*Below left: The remaining strips of embroidery from a bag (see page 50) were stitched onto a piece of velvet from an old child's dress that had been discharge dyed. The cord is made from the same wool as the bag handle – several lengths of cord were zigzag stitched together and these were then applied around the cushion with a further wide zigzag stitch.*

*Below: Attaching cord to cushion edge.*

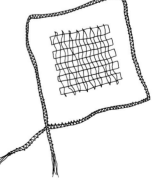

49

*Above: Stitching the zip into the bag with a satin stitch under the machine. Reinforced buttonhole stitch over loops to hold the 'hooks' of the bag handle.*

## PROJECT: MAKE-UP BAG

**You will need::**

- Paper for pattern
- Your piece of pieced-together embroidery fabric
- Lining if preferred
- Zip
- Suitable hand stitching thread for buttonhole stitch
- Suitable thread for machine satin stitch
- Plastic-covered electrical wire

You will require one square of fabric for the base (if you are short of embroidered fabric, this could be something plain, reinforced with pelmet Vylene). For the sides you will need four pieces of the 'arch' shape. This really is a question of cutting your cloth to fit. Whatever size you can fit onto the re-stitched embroidery piece you have will dictate the size of the bag.

You will need a zip the length of two sides of the arch. But you could consider lacing through eyelets or loops, or buttons and loops.

My embroidered pieces were so heavily stitched that adding more satin stitch to them to hold them together seemed appropriate. If this does not fit in with the style of the embroidery, add appropriate seam allowances.

### Technique

1. Stitch two sides of your fabrics together, then the other two sides.
2. Place the zip between the two sides. Again, I did this with a satin stitch but you could do this within a seam allowance if it's more appropriate.
3. Place the four sides on the base of the fabric and stitch the edges together with a satin stitch. For a neat back with seams it might be preferable to cover this afterwards with a binding tape.
4. Several loops of pearl cotton were stitched into the seams of the bag, then overstitched with a reinforced buttonhole stitch.
5. Wrap a piece of 2.5 mm (1 in) plastic-coated electrical wire with left-over knitting wool and hook into the loops.

*Opposite: An embroidery based on a flower garden was cut up into small pieces of about 2.5 cm (1 in) square. With other bits of fabric in harmonious colours these pieces were dabbed lightly with PVA glue and stuck to a background fabric until it was completely covered. The whole surface was stitched with zigzag stitch.*

*Right: a) Pieces for making bag; b) Making the bag; c) Different ideas for closures.*

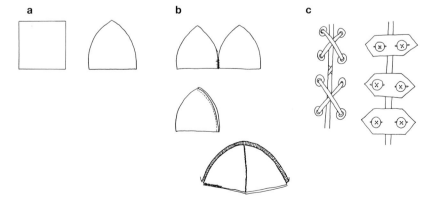

a          b          c

# RECYCLING EMBROIDERIES FROM OTHER CULTURES AND TIMES

Working with or on found embroideries that are not of your own making is a delicate process and one that should be approached with thought and respect for the original work and its intention.

Your choices should be justified by the use to which you will be putting the embroidery in the future. The work may be seen as a comment on the work of the culture and time that you have taken the embroidery from, and you should be clear before you start how you feel about this and whether there are things that you wish to bring to light and interpret. The title that you choose for the work or the references that you choose to make could be of paramount importance. The answer may be simple.

- Perhaps you are influenced by the joy and colours experienced by the original embroiderer, and you wish to take this and add to it in a contemporary way; integrating the whole into a cross-culture or cross-time celebration of embroidery or textile techniques. The work has influenced your own work and its inclusion into your work seems a natural extension of this.
- You may wish to include an old piece with your work simply because it is very beautiful and it lends itself perfectly to the visual impact you are trying to give.
- You may wish to take something with a heavy cultural reference and represent it to make a strong comment. One thinks of Robert Rauchenberg's *Bed* piece,

*Below:* Here Comes the Sun by the author. The title is borrowed from George Harrison after watching images from the first charity concert given for Bangladesh – hence the eastern influence. The base fabric is a sample piece of felt that had been used to demonstrate various methods of applying colour, the chain-stitched Indian embroidery came from an old cushion which fell apart. The metal coils were made cutting pieces from an old copper vent over a gas cooker (the copper was being recycled for etching plates). The small wire coils and glass beads came from a rather nice pendant light. The threads were given to me by my old needlework teacher.

paint worked onto an old log cabin quilt, which makes a comment on American culture in a post-pop art context. For this approach to work, you need to be fully informed about the cultural references and devices used in the original embroidery to be sure that you are capable of making relevant comments or that the comments made are relevant to you. It is always easier to do this in relation to pieces from within our own cultural heritage (whatever we may deem this to be).

- You may wish to use old embroideries to comment on the past life of embroiderers and the past time of embroidery or the inculcation of young girls through embroidery to be content with their lives as servants or to use as objects of decoration within their own home.

- You may wish to comment on the exploitation of workers in the home and in factories at home and abroad in the manufacture of embroidery.

- You may wish to comment or make a memory piece about your own past history, or the past history of your family through the inclusion of embroideries from your family.

- You may wish to comment on embroidery and textiles as an art form throughout history. The re-introduction of patching or embroidery techniques to a contemporary piece can make the viewer appreciate these objects as an art form (at whatever level). You may find something to say about samplers, canvas work, patchwork or even crinoline ladies!

*Below: Old lace handkerchief attached to two pages of a facsimile of* Mrs Beaton's Book of Household Management. *One page talks about friendship – choosing your friends and not purveyors of lies. The other about cleaning techniques (advice for the hanky!). Around the handkerchief the words 'T'is true: there's magic in the web of it' come from Shakespeare's* Othello, *referring to the handkerchief that is the undoing of Desdemona and Othello because of Iago's lies.*

# CHAPTER FOUR
# RECYCLING PAPER AND ORGANIC WASTE

## CREATING PAPERS OUT OF CELLULOSE AND ORGANIC WASTE FOR STITCHING

Paper can be a wonderful surface for embroidery; as it responds to the needle so the surface changes. It can become more fragile through the creation of holes, but with a greater tensile strength as the added threads become interlinked and form a fabric with the paper. By creating your own papers you can recycle old paper, recycle other organic waste and incorporate bits and pieces of thread, leaves, petals, fabrics, and so on, into the construction of the paper to personalize it. You can also sculpt with the finished result or you may even use papier-mâché to make forms from moulds.

Papermaking at home is relatively easy, but does require some equipment and can be messy. So for those who would like the result (or similar) without the mess, here's a solution.

### CHEAT'S PAPER
Here's an easy method of creating a paper while incorporating anything you think fit! You will be able to incorporate flowers, leaves or grasses, bits of fabric or old lace, threads or pieces of metal, plastics or pieces of printed paper. Cheat's paper is quite malleable and very easily stitched into.

*Right: Cheat's paper with hollyhock petals, stitched together with fleece stitch. The colouring comes from the petals.*

Water-dissolvable paper is made from cellulose and will give you cellulose in an easily dissolvable sheet format. All you need to do is to stitch whatever you want onto the paper.

**Technique**

1. Start by simply putting a few petals, leaves or other organic material onto vanishing paper. You can use one layer or two for added cellulose, particularly when adding fabric or metal bits.
2. Stitch over the whole surface with an open fleece stitch, which will show very little in the final paper, but will hold the surface together.
3. In a flat-bottomed bowl about the same size as the paper, place the work on a piece of nylon chiffon or organdie (cotton, silk or synthetic). Pour in just enough water for the paper to soak it all up.
4. Agitate the work with your fingers, rubbing into the dissolvable paper to work the cellulose into a gel-like pulp.
5. Once this is all dissolved into a pulp, pull the paper out of the bowl with the fabric underneath it.

*Below: Cheat's paper with lace and petal inclusions, coloured with bronze powders and machine embroidered.*

*Right: Rose petals on dissolvable paper before dissolving.*

6.   Put it onto a surface (a wooden board) to dry. You can at this stage add other fibres, flowers or bits and pieces into the pulp. The drying process can take some time (days), so if there were any moulds in the objects you incorporated into your paper, your paper will go mouldy. If it does, you can treat it with bleach or, if you are worried about this, dry it with a hairdryer. The paper can equally be moulded into a form at this wet stage, if you wish.

7.   Gently pull off the fabric backing; the fleece stitch should be hardly visible.

8.   The resulting paper can be stitched into, dyed, painted or added to as you wish. The fabric that you placed underneath may have received some colour, or have bits stuck to it, and you may find a use for this too in your embroidery.

## PROJECT: CHEAT'S PAPER BOWL OR FORM

Follow steps 1 to 6 (above). You can now place this paper over a mould such as a balloon, which can be gently let down once the paper is dry, or into a mould from which you will be able to detach it once it's dry – a relatively flexible plastic bowl or mould will be best. The paper will shrink a little as it dries, so don't place it over a rigid mould.

## THE VERY BASICS OF PAPERMAKING

The best papers are made from long fibres, but the problems of recycling existing cotton fibres into paper requires the use of specialized machinery and is not the aim of this book.

Cotton linters can be bought in sheet form and can be used for papermaking. Although this is not recycling in itself, these linters can give added strength to any paper made from recycled paper or other organic material. This is particularly true when recycling newspaper, which can be very fragile owing to the chemical processes involved in its manufacture and the shortness of the fibres used. The cotton linters can be used in quantities as little as 20 per cent to add strength, or up to 50 per cent, which will affect the overall finish.

*Below:* Rose Bowl. *Rose petals were stitched onto two layers of vanishing paper. This was then carefully dissolved onto a net backing which was formed into a bowl to dry and then coloured with oil pastels.*

**You will need:**

- Old newspaper
- Bowls or buckets to soak the 'ingredients' for your paper
- Blender – an ordinary domestic blender is ideal for making pulp
- Vat to mix the pulp with water: this needs to be large and flat – at least twice as large as your mould
- Mould and deckle (The mould is a wire mesh-covered frame used to scoop up pulp from the vat. The deckle is an empty frame that sits on top of the mould and this will shape and form the edges of the paper. These can be purchased at many craft suppliers in different sizes, or for your first attempts you can simply use a fat splash guard used to protect frying pans).
- Felt (The wet paper is transferred to a felt surface once made. You can use anything cheap that you have to hand – kitchen cloths, non-woven fabrics, even woven fabrics – this will give a surface pattern to your paper)
- Pressing boards (any board will do) for squeezing out excess water to speed the drying process
- Old towels for mopping up as papermaking is wet and messy!

**Technique**

1. You will need a basic cellulose mix. For old newspaper, tear it into about 2 cm (¾ in) square strips and soak for about one hour. For cotton linters, soak overnight, and then tear into small pieces as above. Either of these can be mixed into a pulp with lots of water in your blender. Pay careful attention to the blender so that it doesn't overheat. Only work in short bursts, and use lots of water in the mix. For fine paper the pulp should be lump free when finished, but you may prefer to keep some texture. If you are using newspaper some pieces with the printed word may still be visible if you don't mash it too much.
2. Add the pulp to the vat with lots more water to make a thin cream consistency.
3. In one continuous movement, dip the mould (with deckle in place if you are using one), vertically into the vat, then into a horizontal position. Raise it carefully taking the pulp evenly across the surface and allow the water to drain out over the vat.
4. The mould should then be turned through 360 degrees and the paper laid (couched – from the French word *couché*) onto the felt with a little knock. If you are not happy with the result you can scoop up the pulp, put it back into the vat and try again. A useful tip, if you don't manage to 'couch' your paper, is to cut the felt into the right size to fit your frame, and even a board the same size. You can then place the felt onto the paper and squeeze out some of the water with the board at this stage. Now when you turn the frame over, it should come away onto the felt, or you can peel it off. Rubbing the back of the metal grid can also help to release the paper.
5. You can press the paper by layering between felts – place several pieces of paper one on top of the other, interleaved with felt, in between two boards. By standing on them, or placing a weight on top, you will expel some of the water.

Place towels underneath or work outside. If the paper is well pressed, you can hang it up to dry at this stage. If you don't wish to press the paper, you can leave it to dry flat in the air – although as this can take a long time, be smelly and there is a risk of mould, you may wish to speed up the drying process by placing the paper in a warm airy place.

## MAKING PAPER WITH OTHER INGREDIENTS

There are many recipes for making paper with all sorts of organic material, and all kinds of colourings such as spices, dyes, or incorporating a small amount of commercially coloured paper with your pulp. Try some of the following and then experiment yourself:

- Cut small bits of left-over fabric and thread bits into small lengths and include them in your pulp (once made and in the vat), so that they form in a haphazard fashion on the paper, or add them into the paper afterwards, while still very wet and in the frame. String, thread and fabric bits can also be included between two pieces of wet formed paper.
- Whizz some washed autumn leaves in the blender: fill the blender a quarter full with leaves and top up to halfway with water. Use short bursts to be able to stop the blender at the desired consistency. This mixture can then be added to paper pulp. This very simple method can be used for much organic waste such as leaves and flowers.
- Some items would be best boiled, particularly grass, to avoid moulds. Place cut grass in a stainless steel saucepan. Cover well with water and boil for an hour. The result can make a very thick grass paper – for show or stitching, not for writing on! Mix a small amount of the grass with pre-soaked newspaper or linters in the blender. The chlorophyll from the grass will really colour your paper nicely.

*Below: Grass paper with zigzag stitching in a multi-colour thread. It has been backed with a piece of stiff muslin that has already been used for cleaning etching plates and so is coloured with ink.*

## MAKING A CAUSTIC SOLUTION

Some items can be boiled in a caustic solution to boil down the cellulose and make a finer paper. You can use caustic soda or make your own caustic solution as follows:

1.  Fill about a third of a stainless steel saucepan with wood ash. Then fill up to the two-thirds mark with water.
2.  Boil for about one hour.
3.  Strain off any bits then pass through a fine sieve.

You can use this solution mixed with a little more water to boil down the cellulose fibres in many plants to make paper, using the resulting pulp with or without additional paper or cotton pulp.

A diluted version will give you skeleton leaves – remove them carefully and wash them after boiling. Excess leaf pulp can be scraped away from the veins with a spoon or blunt knife.

If you have just a small amount of a particular pulp, you can pour it directly onto your mould from a jug and just collect the water underneath in the vat. Try to spread out the pulp as evenly as possible as you are pouring it into the mould, or use a spoon. Work as quickly as possible while the pulp is still very wet. (See *Venetian Window with Blue Shutters* on page 18 for paper made with autumn leaves using this method.)

*Below:* Along the Grand Canal, Venice *by the author. Machine stitching with different thread thickness on silk paper on a pulp and autumn-leaf paper base. The paper base had been treated with bronze paint and patina fluid.*

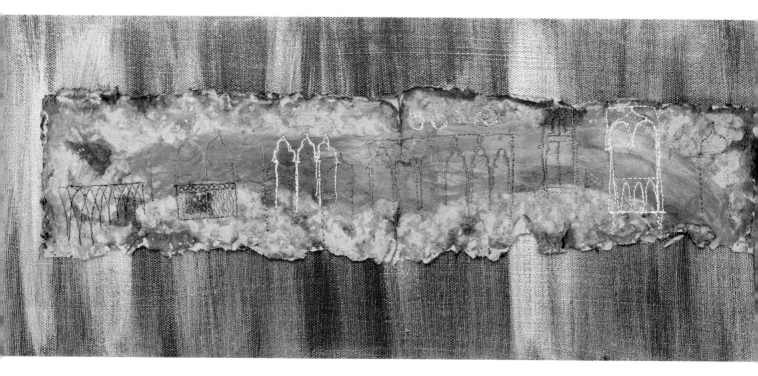

## COLOURING

If you have not included small bits of coloured paper or other colouring matter into your paper, you can colour your paper afterwards with all your favourite colouring methods. You will find that water-based paint will just get soaked up into the paper unless you have sized it or included a glue (wallpaper paste) in it. Long-fibred papers (including cotton) will react better to water-based mediums than other types. Acrylic paints and oil pastels will be fine. The interesting textures of some cruder papers can work well with bronzing powders in acrylic wax or patina paints, which give the appearance of metal with a patina in blue or green verdigris. These products are available with a variety of metal colours as the base coat and with several different colours as false verdigris.

### Technique

1.  Shake the bottle of metallic base coat until it no longer makes a noise. It really does need a good shake.
2.  Apply one coat and allow to it dry.
3.  Apply a second coat.
4.  While it is still tacky, apply the patina top coat using a soft brush. You will need to experiment to become familiar with the results you can get. If you apply too much of everything you can get some crackling (which is nice), but you may be disappointed if the surface is all-over verdigris with very little metal showing through. If your paper is moulded, you could restrict your application of the patina to the high moulded areas only, to give a realistic effect.

Instead of the prescribed metallic bases, bronzing powders in acrylic wax work very well and give a beautiful colour – the result is less 'encrusted'. Apply the patina fluid while the bronzing powders are still tacky.

## PAPIER-MÂCHÉ WITH PAPER AND TEXTILES INCORPORATED

Making papier-mâché forms is pretty easy using any paper, whether it is old or new – you can even use your own handmade papers.

### MOULDS

For an open shape you can work onto any mould, but it can be a little tricky unsticking your papier-mâché object from the mould. Covering the mould with petroleum jelly or silicone spray first can help, or you can use a balloon as a mould and simply deflate it once the work is dry. You could also create the desired shape in close-formed chicken wire or something similar first, then work your papier-mâché onto both sides of that.

If you are creating a solid shape, you can even use pre-soaked newspaper as for papermaking: add one part PVA to the water, and sculpt with this as a starting point (as long as it's not too thick), adding papier mâché strips to it afterwards.

CREATING THE SURFACE

Tear the paper into small pieces: you can use small squares of about 2–5 cm (¾–2 in) or long thin strips, depending on the type of mould you are trying to cover. You may wish to use smallish pieces to build up a surface that is well integrated.

You can use bigger strips for the first and final layers to create movement or textural interest – particularly if you are using a special paper. If the strips are too big or stiff to lie flat, you can place pieces of fine tissue paper over the first layer, as your second layer, before continuing, or as a fine final layer, if your last layer is stiff and difficult.

Work about 6–10 layers onto the mould by positioning the paper, then working adhesive into it with a brush. You can use one part PVA to one part water. With larger or firmer pieces of paper, you might find it advantageous to dip them into your PVA mix (I have mine on a plate) and then place them on the mould, if the pieces are large, stiff or unruly.

Once you have finished, leave the piece to dry before detaching carefully from the mould.

**Ideas**

*Below: Papier-mâché bowl made with stitched leftover paper and a piece of embroidery cut off the edge of a 'failure'.*

- Include dry organic waste in the first or final layers, such as dried flowers, herbs, leaves, grasses and bark.
- Include fresh organic waste such as grass cutting, or fresh petals or leaves. For fresh grass, which rots easily, you could boil it for an hour first as with papermaking, so that it is bacteria free.

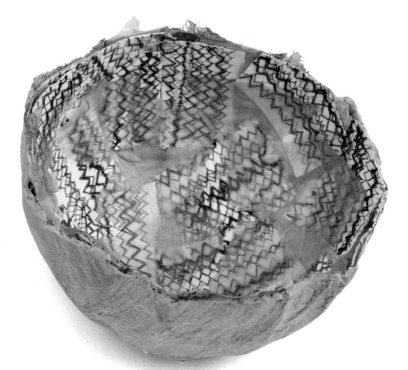

- Try including small snippets of thread or pieces of fabric – particularly in the first and final layers, so that they can be seen.
- Try stitching on the paper first before incorporating it. You can run all over the paper with a machine zigzag. To create texture, try using threads of different thickness – some slightly thicker threads such as Madeira wool or hand weaver's studio silk or rayon can run through topstitch needles with a zero top tension on some machines – or use two threads in the needles at once. You could include stitching worked with cable stitch or apply ribbons or cords. Once your paper is stitched and textured, cut it into pieces. If it is worked on a fine supple paper, you should have no difficulties. If you have used a thicker paper for your experiments, see page 62 for incorporating stiff papers into your papier-mâché form.
- Try incorporating old textiles or failed cut-up bits of embroidery into your papier-mâché (see chapter 3).
- Try using your own handmade papers, interesting bought long-fibre papers, left-over bits, wrapping paper and so on.
- You can use quite stiff papers – off-cuts from framing of watercolour or drawing papers. I find it best in this case to use one layer of thicker paper, followed by a layer of thinner paper. You can build up a form in as few as six layers.
- When colouring the final piece, you could allow these pieces to show through by simply glazing over the final piece with acrylic glaze or more PVA.
- Use a diluted paint solution (acrylic or ink would be best) to bring all the colours together while allowing the inclusions to show.
- Use a tissue paper as your final layer so that trapped pieces underneath it show through.
- If inclusions are simply textural – the type of paper used, pieces of lace, flowers or leaves that offer a texture to the surface – you could rub in bronzing powders with a brush, or oil pastels can be rubbed over the surface to accentuate the texture. If you have used oil pastel, the rest can be painted with a water-based paint, which will resist the oil or wax crayons already rubbed into the surface.
- Papers can be coloured with any of your favourite colouring mediums, from watercolour and inks, dyes, acrylic paint, bronzing powders, to wax and oil pastels (these can be ironed afterwards to become really imbedded into the fibres of the paper) and gilding wax. Try different methods of colouring before and after stitching to see the different effects.

STITCHING
- You can hand stitch into the surface of your papier-mâché. If it is a little hard, use an awl to gently make the holes for your stitching.
- The surface will be a little hard for machining, but you could have machined over the paper to be included in the first or final surfaces first in order to create a texture before inclusion.

# INCORPORATING ORGANIC MATERIALS INTO EMBROIDERY AND EMBROIDERY INTO ORGANIC MATERIALS

Including found organic materials in your work is a good way to make a statement, perhaps about the nature of where the objects came from or what they actually mean to you – perhaps a memory of a garden or of a certain time or space.

Organic materials may also be incorporated simply because they provide the right kind of textural interest to the work. Skeleton leaves, flower heads, dried grasses and so on, can all bring a textural interest to a piece of work, as well as making comments about the environment.

We've already looked at many ways of incorporating organic materials into fibre surfaces and paper, so let's look at incorporating them with stitch and fabric.

**Ideas**

- Stitching through organic materials can sometimes be rather delicate, particularly on the machine. Objects can be treated with a PVA thinned with water to help hold them together during stitching.
- Consider carefully the use of stitch. Do you want it to be decorative, very visible or part of the design?
- Stitching should be subtle if you want it to integrate well into the surfaces being stitched. Consider using invisible thread if you don't want your stitching to stand out and be seen.
- Try to avoid the areas that are most delicate and likely to fall apart, stitching over stems rather than through flowers for example.
- To hold delicate pieces in place while stitching, place a fine Aquafilm over the surface of your work and gently dissolve it afterwards. Using bonding powder or adhesive webbing can also be a solution. PVA used too thickly may cause problems for your stitching if you are using a machine.
- Trap organic objects between see-through net, organdie or fine chiffon.
- Synthetic fabrics respond well to cutting with heat. Use a soldering iron or joss stick to make holes to allow the flowers, seeds or leaves to peep through.
- Butter muslin is a very 'close to nature' sort of fabric, which may be appropriate to your work, and it can be pulled into holes easily with your fingers or with stitched pulled work by hand or machine. Again, these holes can be used to reveal what is underneath.
- Working with open-weave fabrics, you could thread or weave grasses or stems into the material or wrap stems or sticks with thread and weave them together.
- Buttonhole stitch or needle-made lace can be used over items too delicate or hard to stitch, in order to hold them down.
- Machine-made laces on vanishing fabric could be used similarly.
- As well as the appearance of the work, you might consider smell – some plants and flowers can hold their perfume for some time.

*Below: The paper for the papier-mâché bowl (see page 62) was stitched before being cut up and used for the bowl.*

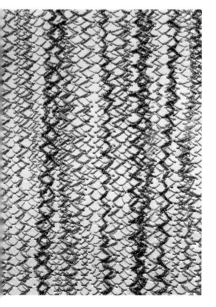

**DRYING FLOWERS**

You can dry flowers simply by hanging them up in a warm place, where there is a reasonable current of air. An airing cupboard can work well too, simply because the flowers will dry so rapidly that there will be no danger of moulds forming. Some flowers can even be dried in a few minutes in a warm oven. Not all flowers dry well, particularly if they are very moist, so it may be best to separate the petals and dry them individually. Petals and whole flowers can look pretty included in embroideries, paper, silk paper and vanishing fabric laces. With techniques that involve water (paper, cheat's paper, dissolvable fabric), their colours may bleed, so either check this first, or take this into account when designing.

**SKELETON LEAVES**

Creating skeleton leaves is a relatively hit-and-miss affair as all leaves require different soaking times or cooking times to achieve a skeleton quality.

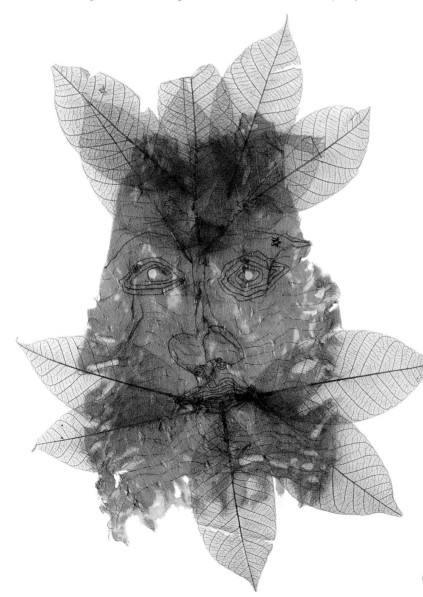

*Left:* Green Man II *by Julieanne Long, made from a small piece of metallic fabric, wire and skeleton leaves. The shape of the face was built up with stitching fuse wire into fabric and manipulating it. The features were stitched and the piece singed with a hot air gun. The skeleton leaves were added at the end.*

65

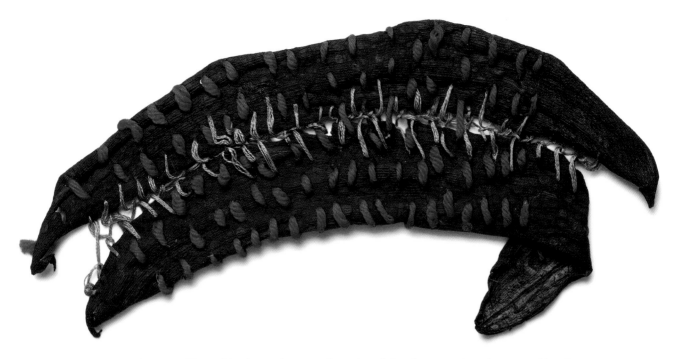

Try soaking leaves in a caustic soda solution for several weeks, or cooking them for 30–60 minutes. Make up the solution with 100 g (3½ oz) of washing soda (sodium carbonate) to 3 litres (105½ fl oz) of water. Sodium carbonate can be bought in a purer form as PH Plus for swimming pools. The advantage of soaking leaves is that the process is slow, so you should be able to catch them at the right stage of decay. With cooking, the results happen fast and it's very easy to overdo it.

**Technique**

1. In a saucepan, fill to a third with wood ash, then fill to two-thirds with water and boil for one hour. Strain off and use the liquid as a caustic solution to boil leaves. Boil for about 30 minutes and check regularly for the result. If you overdo it, the ending mash can always be used for making paper!

2. Once the flesh of the leaf is soft, you can start to pull it away from the leaf skeleton with a toothbrush or a fine sharp object. If you want to, you can bleach the leaf skeletons afterwards with a diluted solution of bleach. You may hit on the right combination of circumstances for a particular leaf type, and then have to experiment again for a different leaf, adding or taking away from the time or the concentration of caustic soda, according to the quality of the leaf.

STITCHING

Skeleton leaves are fragile but can be stitched with fine thread by hand or machine. For machine stitching use largish stitches, around 3–4 mm (¼ in) to avoid causing too many perforations. They can be applied to work or included in papermaking or vanishing fabric, but dissolve the work carefully.

Stitching on fresh leaves is very interesting and worth exploiting. If you stitch over the surface of the leaves, the amount of perforations seem to speed up the drying out process and the leaf doesn't rot, but dries out instead. I experimented using natural fibres for the stitching, assuming that these might help with the drying.

**SEAWEED**

Drying seaweed is fairly easy. You may simply wash it and dry it in a warm place in a through current of air. However, you can also dry it in a press, which may make it easier to use in your work. The colours will be maintained.

**Technique**

1. Wash the seaweed and sandwich it between layers of kitchen towel and old fabrics such as felt or dishcloths.
2. Press under a press or heavy book until it's dry. Check from time to time that it is drying well, and is not mouldy. You can change the kitchen towel and clothes that immediately touch it if necessary.
3. You will need to wash the clothes thoroughly afterwards, as they can take on the smell of the seaweed. The resulting seaweed should not be smelly. The drying process can take weeks depending on the drying environment.

# EARTHWORKS

Textile artists have also turned their attention to land art and earthworks, stitching into the ground, working with wood and weaving, creating patterns and stitches or the appearance of stitches with grass or other natural material, found objects, stone or sand. The work may be time-based or permanent, be presented in indoor or outdoor environments, or simply as a collection of photographs recording the event. The important element in all such work is the concept underlying the event or construction, which needs to be strong and well thought out. The visual effect can be stunning, as textile art and embroidery are not expected to appropriate nature in an intervening and imposing way, but are more usually expected to echo it through delicate reproduction.

*Left: Sculpture made from beach combings by Michel Arnaud.*

# CHAPTER FIVE

# RECYCLING PLASTIC WASTE

Most people would agree that far too much plastic is created and thrown away. Recycling is a necessary solution if our countryside is not to become littered and unsightly, causing a danger to ourselves and to wildlife. Plastic recycled in textile art and embroidery can be used to make this statement. Also it can quite simply be used as the appropriation of an interesting surface for the texture and decorative possibilities that it can bring to a work. For whatever reason these surfaces are employed, these days we find more and more plastic included in textile art and embroidery.

**Notes:**
- For the following ideas and experiments use as fine a needle as possible (topstitch or embroidery if working on the machine).
- When heat treating plastic surfaces use a mask and work in a well-ventilated area, as plastics can give off toxic or unpleasant fumes.
- If you are using an iron, place the plastic between two sheets of baking parchment (silicone or Teflon paper), and look regularly to see the effect – it will be different on the reverse side to the side you are ironing.
- If you are using a heat tool, work on a fireproof surface and work near a source of water or a bowl of water.

## INCLUDING PLASTICS IN EMBROIDERY

**Ideas**
- Plastics can offer a range of interesting surfaces when added to and integrated into embroideries worked by hand or machine.
- Bits of shiny plastic can be left showing through heavy areas of stitching.
- Heat treating plastics can create melted or formed, textured or bubbled surfaces that can respond well to stitching and create real areas of interest and texture within the work.
- Fine plastic pulled or cut into long threads can be used for stitching or couched down onto a surface.
- Plastic pieces can be pieced together to make a patchwork surface. The patchwork could then be embroidered.
- Bits and pieces can be trapped under transparent plastic forming pockets within a work.

*Left: Patchwork by Patricia Hann made by weaving plastic carrier bags into a prepared warp of odd bits of wool. The squares are cut, sewn into and reassembled to make a patchwork. Inspired by an exhibition of Third World craft and reusing plastic bags to make three-dimensional objects, this piece brings home the notion of how much of what the West throws away would be put to use elsewhere.*

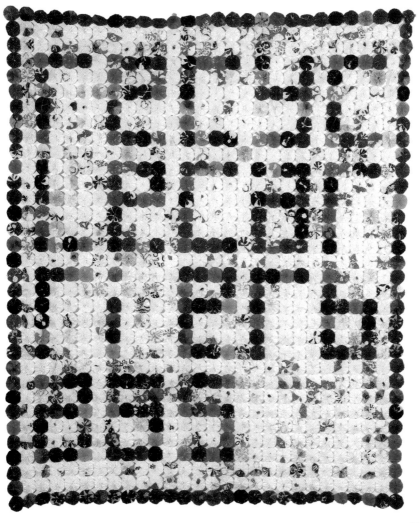

*Left:* Recycle Carrier Bags *by Lynn Setterington. Handmade Suffolk puffs using supermarket/grocery bags. 'This quilt is one in a series and is a comment on both our throwaway culture, where everything is disposable and nothing is made to last, as well as the power and dominance of the big supermarkets and our supermarket-shopping culture. The ubiquitous carriers are transformed to circles of pattern and colour, constructed to convey a simple message to the viewer. My interest in historical quilts and textiles is shown here – the date of construction, as well as the social status of the quilt maker, can be determined by the fabrics used.'*

*Above:* Missmots *by Fanny Violet. Taillefine is a make of low-calorie, low-fat, processed food, which translates into a thin waist. Missmots is about 30 cm (11¾ in) high.*

## INCLUDING EMBROIDERY IN DIFFERENT PLASTIC SURFACES

Working into plastic as the medium in itself, rather than just using it as an addition to other materials can be interesting too.

**Ideas**
- Too much stitching may cause the plastic to disintegrate or change shape. Experiment with disintegration and the manipulation of the surface through the stitches used.
- Machine stitch in different directions and with different densities.
- With hand stitching use the manipulative possibilities of running stitch – pull the stitching a little as you go.
- Use transparent plastic and trap things within it before adding further stitching. To trap between two pieces of plastic, use the heat of an iron. Try plastic file holders, kitchen plastic wrap, clear plastic bags or decorative plastic such a florist's wrapping. The result could then be stitched on, or cut into pieces and applied to another surface for embroidery

### HEAT TREATMENT FOR SURFACES
Heat treating plastics can be unsafe, so please follow the notes and advice at the start of this chapter for your own protection, and never work for long periods at a time. Stop if you start to feel unwell or dizzy, or if the smell or smoke seems very unpleasant. Always have water handy. Collect a quantity of plastics from different sources and try the following:
- Tyvek can be included in these experiments. Different qualities of Tyvek are found in envelopes, emergency clothing and the building trade. Cut the plastic into 25 cm (10 in) square pieces for the experiments. This will help you gauge shrinkage, but will give you pieces big enough to use for embroidery experiments should you wish to.
- Experiment with different iron temperatures on different plastics – note the difference between the top and the reverse of each of the plastics.

- Experiment with a heat tool at different powers and distances on different plastics and note the difference between the top and the reverse side.
- Use the heat on the different plastics until they start to melt or holes are created.
- With each of the pieces created try out embroidery stitches and techniques to see how they could be integrated into work as added texture. Try hand or machine stitching, and machine tension techniques such as whip stitch, feather stitch or cable.
- Try fusing plastics together using heat, or rolling or moulding plastics and heat setting them.

Working with heat and plastics has become something of a phenomenon in current embroidery practice – it's worth looking at the large and impressive destructive/deconstruction pieces of holed burned plastic made by the Italian artist Alberto Burri in the 1960s to see some of the origins of this kind of approach. The sometimes violent nature of bringing this work into being has perhaps something more to say about us and our environment than we care to admit when we are creating these intriguing surfaces. While you are researching Alberto Burri, you will also notice his recycling of Burlap flour and grain bags into painter's canvas at a time when he couldn't get hold of any other surfaces to paint on (he was a prisoner of war).

*Below:* Survival Corset *by Eva Demarelatrous, part of a series of work on the body. Seeds, vegetables, herbs, spices and coffee are layered in between two layers of agricultural plastic. One could either eat or plant the contents.*

*Above right:* The Day the Earth Caught Fire *by the author with daughters Lucy and Joanne (aged 12 and 8). The title comes from a 1960s disaster movie, although the subject is global warming. The polystyrene pieces were first glued onto a 'disposable' (sic) cleaning cloth, then ironed, and painted with acrylic paint.*
*Finally it was hand and machine stitched with feather stitching. The piece was burned around the edge using a candle flame with a bowl of water to extinguish the cloth when it was burned enough.*

## HARDER PLASTICS

Perspex of different thickness and the plastic offered frequently instead of glass for framing can be stitched on and included in your work or used as a support for embroidery. Cutting the finer plastic is easy with a modelling knife – just score it a couple of times and then bend it. Thicker perspex is more difficult. If you cannot get it cut professionally you will have to resort to using an electric jigsaw and then sand the edges afterwards. Protect the parts you are going to cut with masking tape. Holes can be made for stitching with a soldering iron. Do this in a well-ventilated space and wear a mask. Any thicker plastic you find that is too hard for a needle to make holes, will probably respond to a soldering iron, although this makes hand stitching a better option than machine stitching. However, it does not stop you hand stitching machine-stitched pieces or laces to the plastic.

## BEACH COMBING

Beach combing should perhaps come under the heading of wood and minerals, but unfortunately these days, and I'm sure the avid beach combers will agree, most of the things we find on the beach are plastic, although washed up wood and drink cans still do feature. Ropes, sandals, string, bags, plastic bottles, bottle tops and so on are destroyed very little by their time spent in the waves and litter the shores with their bright colours. Working them into pictures and sculptures is a way of giving them a more useful future.

Constructing with glue or stitching on or combining them with other found pieces take us back to the sea and beach-combing days. Including pebbles or sand, wave-washed wood and other flotsam and jetsam can feel nostalgic.

*Below:* Beach Cords *by Michel Arnaud, part of a series of canvases made uniquely with coloured cords found on beaches.*

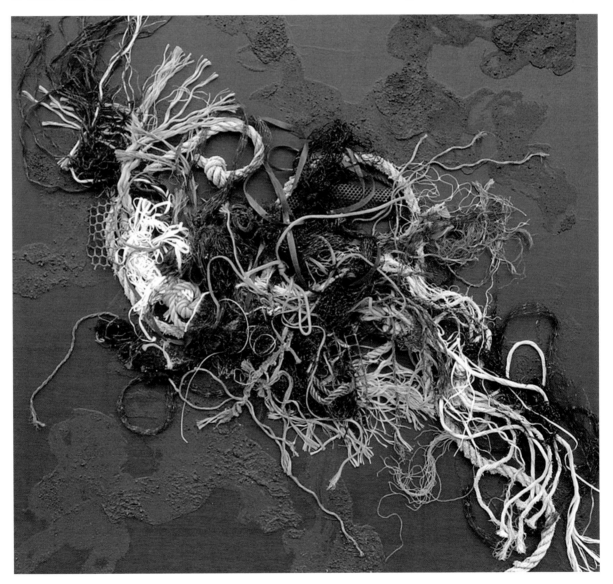

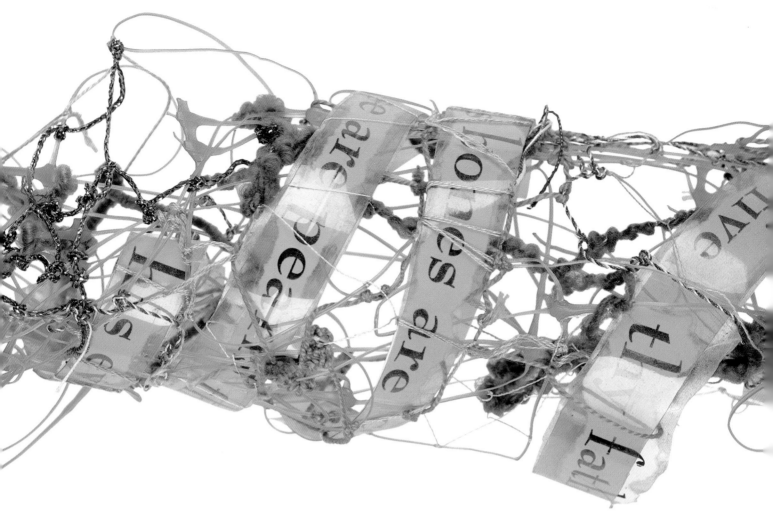

## WEAVING AND FUSION TO CREATE TACTILE PIECES WITH FIBRE INCLUSION

Plastic surfaces such as plastic bags can be very suitable for cutting into strips for weaving, knitting, crochet or coarse stitching. Threads and other fibres can be included. The resulting surface can be heat fused for permanence or flattened by heat once created, and could be stitched into by hand or machine for further decoration.

### Ideas

- Plastic bottles could be cut down to the bottom (lengthways into narrow strips), and textiles or other plastics woven in and out of these strips.
- Plastic bottles cut be cut in the round and involved in sculptural work.
- Try knitting, crochet or weaving with old cassette tape. Your tension must be loose as the tape is fragile if pulled too hard. Once made, try ironing the surface to fuse it – it will flatten and stick lightly itself. Try stitching on it – don't over do it – the tape is quite fragile. Try including other threads as you knit.
- Try knitting or crochet with cut lengths of plastic bags. When cutting up the plastic bags, try to cut a continuous strip so that knitting is easier. You can do this by cutting across the bag diagonally as if you are making a bias strip.
- Collect different coloured bags and try weaving them on a simple frame. You could start the warp with plastic lengths or strong threads, and weave

the plastic in and out in a simple weave, or create a tapestry weave with the different colours.

- Working on a coarse rug canvas or metal grid, try stitching with lengths of plastic using a large tapestry needle. Experiment with different stitches.
- If you have stitched on rug canvas, you could try machine stitching into the surface to flatten the texture in some areas, or fuse the work with an iron.
- Working on a metal grid with the canvas work, you could try shaping it or fusing the plastic.

*Above: Weaving plastic*

*Left: Knitted and fused cassette tape with some zigzag stitching.*

*Below: Knitted cassette tape before ironing*

# CHAPTER SIX
## RECYCLING WOOD, METAL AND MINERAL WASTE

### RECYCLING CANS AND METAL

*Below: Full Circle by Mary Crehan. The heart is made from papier-mâché and covered in dyed fabric, with tubes and old TV cables wrapped in red and blue wools.*

Adding metal threads, colour, fabric or specially purchased metals and meshes to your embroidery, or working into these surfaces can be costly, and much suitable material is just thrown away. By beating cans or metal tubes flat you will find a surface suitable for machine embroidery. Metal meshes exist in all sorts of functions and may be suitable for hand or machine stitching, and if you take old engine bits, televisions or other paraphernalia apart, you may well find wires or copper coils just waiting for a new lease of life. Use protective gloves, wire cutters, pliers or old scissors to help you make the most of what you find, and take care to correctly dispose of anything you choose not to keep.

## MACHINE EMBROIDERY INTO METAL

Any quality sewing machine will be able to embroider through thin metal, such as cans and the sort of metal you find in tomato paste tubes. The needle will be no good for anything else afterwards, however, so keep one especially for this kind of work. The threads will cut on the underside of the metal if it is not backed with something. You can use any firm fabric as a backing, but if you use a firm vanishing fabric such as Solusheet or vanishing paper, you will be able to dissolve this backing afterwards leaving only the metal surface. This is useful if you wish to exploit the metal quality for sculpture or jewellery, rather than just as an applied material.

*Above: Stitch on the metal foil found in a wine box. The 'fabric' was first stitched through all its layers (two of foil and two of plastic interior) to give a quilted effect. I deemed it too shiny, so took the shine off with further stitching. The triangles are stitched with cable stitch.*

*Left:* All Washed Up *by the author. This coke can, found washed up on the beach and very wave-battered, was easy to stitch on.*

## METAL PATCHWORK

Cut open old cans or metal tubes using an old pair of scissors or metal shears and beat them flat. This beating process may soften up any metal that's a bit too hard. Then cut the metal into suitable shapes using the scissors.

Attach the metal piece by piece with free machine embroidery or straight stitching to a firm backing surface. The pieces should be large enough to hold down firmly, otherwise the needle will catch in them and the thread will keep breaking. Stitching the pieces to the surface with a foot and feed-dog up with straight stitch, zigzag or preset embroidery stitches causes fewer problems on stiff metal cans, and you can add free machine embroidery afterwards if you wish too. It is advisable to avoid having more than one thickness of metal can – create a style of patchwork where the cans just touch each other, as this will be easier to stitch.

You can stitch them onto a firm surface that will become part of the work, such as a felt or stiff cotton, or onto vanishing paper or Solusheet, so that the resulting metal surface is free to move. For *Full Metal Bodice* (opposite) I used vanishing paper and placed a piece of Solusheet under this too, to help prevent thread breakage.

If you wish to mould the metal into a shape, it is probably best to do this as you go, unless the shape can be cut and moulded, so choose a shape that you will be able to stitch into. The backing fabric may already be stitched and moulded into this shape – in the case of a garment for example. Extra embroidery can be added to the surface once the patchwork is complete.

*Right:* Coke Can *by Julieanne Long. 'This was an exercise in contrasting surfaces. I found the can in the gutter, squashed. I loved the texture of the surface and used the can to print with (that's why it is pink!) I then made a row of holes across it using a hammer and a large nail. Next, thick wool was stitched and tied to form a row of knots with long ends. These ends were fluffed up using a wire brush.'*

## METAL APPLIQUÉ

Metal pieces can be applied to any firm fabric surface for added shine or to give support to a surface that you wish to sculpt.

### Ideas

- Cut the metal into the desired shapes and attach to the surface of the fabric using free machine embroidery or normal straight stitching.
- If the fabric isn't firm enough to prevent the top thread breaking on the underside of the metal surface, use a vanishing fabric backing (such as Solusheet) on the punched holes made by the needle.
- Including metal strips in the embroidery of a surface can be useful if you wish to form it into a three-dimensional shape. This could be particularly interesting with vanishing fabrics to help keep the form of a lacy structure.
- The shine of the metal surface can be reduced by using very heavy stitching; this could be done with or without thread in the needle – the punched holes can give an interesting effect without thread.
- The shine or colour on the metal surface can also be changed through heating. Here, slow heating over a gas flame will produce the best results, but try different methods to suit you. Hold the metal in pincers as it will get hot.

*Below:* Full Metal Bodice *by the author. Patchwork of soft drink cans worked on solusheet and vanishing paper with an automatic vermicelli stitch. The ring pulls become lace hole, and the lace for lacing is electrical earth wire – the colours go rather well! Around the bottom I included all the bar codes, and various words such as 'can' or 'ice' turn up here and there, as well as ingredients lists and calorie and diet advice. The sexy image of a bodice becomes hardened and dangerous but, in some way, still has to be paid for.*

*Below: Close up of* Full Metal Bodice.

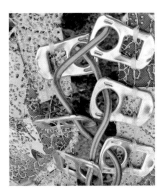

## METAL COILS

Certain metal shears will create coils of metal as they cut through the surface, especially on thicker metals. These can be used for appliqué and inclusion in your embroidery surfaces. They could be attached with hand stitches or applied by machine. Such metal coils may be rather hard, so avoid stitching through them with the machine needle; use a zigzag stitch or satin-stitch blocks to hold them down.

Metal coils can also be made by cutting thin strips of fine metal and coiling them around the end of a pencil or similar object. You may also use electrical wire. This could be stitched down with satin-stitch blocks or hand stitching.

*Right:* Broken Wings *by the author. Repeated images of broken angel wings attached to a painted artists canvas. The first layer is moulded papier-mâché coloured with gold bronzing powders, but verdigris is beginning to attack. The next layer is made from heated tomato paste tubes stitched with free-motion machine embroidery. The final wings are stitched on an embroidery machine using a Sfumato program. The image is taken from angel wings in a church. The piece was worked onto Solusheet dissolvable fabric, then re-stitched with free motion stitching in small circles to ensure that the lacy structure held together. Areas were left unstitched so that the wings would be 'broken'. Hand stitching and soldering residue complete the piece.* Broken Wings *comes from 'Blackbird: Take your broken wings and learn to fly' by Paul McCartney – a song written in celebration of the civil rights movement in the USA.*

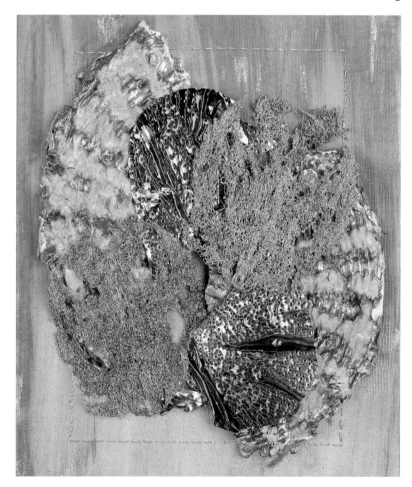

## ELECTRICAL WIRE

This comes in varying thickness, some even fine enough to embroider with by hand, or in the bobbin of the machine. Others are suitable for wrapping by hand or with a machine zigzag stitch. The more current types for household use may have a plastic coating that can be removed easily. Special pliers exist to take off the plastic coating in long pieces and you may even find you can include these in your work as bright-coloured, plastic beads.

- Do be careful when stitching over wire with your machine. It's best not to stitch too fast. If you hit a thick wire at speed with the machine needle it could break; if you are working at a slow to medium speed, there is a good chance that the needle will slide off the wire into the work, or the machine may block and stop. If you are working over very fine wire, and the needle hits the wire, the needle won't break, but it can take the metal thread down with it into the bobbin casing. You will need to stop immediately and retrieve the wire before continuing.

**Ideas**

- If you try using very fine metal wire in the bobbin, use cable stitch settings or bypass the bobbin spring altogether and start off slowly to see if your machine will take it. Your machine may prefer to stitch in a forward direction rather than backwards and forwards (owing to the position of the bobbin case). Work on vanishing fabrics to create interesting laces.
- Wrap metal wire with hand or machine stitching and use in coils or cords.

*Above: Stitching down wire with zigzag and satin-stitch blocks.*

*Left: 'Sugar bowl' made with Romeo dissolvable fabric (Solusheet also works) to give firmness to the bowl structure. The stitching was done first – a spiral, the circles joining the spiral together. If you use metallic thread, use one thread (top or bottom) that is cotton so that it retains the residue for firmness. Four pieces of zigzagged covered wire were added afterwards, finishing in the centre and the outside to form the legs and decoration. It was then dissolved in just a little water, to keep as much residue as possible, and dried over a bowl.*

*Above:* Leaf Bracelet *by Val Woods, inspired by small ivy leaves running along their stem in autumn. The leaves were stitched first, then the wire was applied, and the beads attached by machine after being threaded loosely onto a long thread.*

- If you string beads together you will be able to incorporate the string of beads with a zigzag stitch.
- Include wire with zigzag or satin stitching into vanishing fabric structures – bowls, leaves, flowers, hats, jewellery – for firmness and form. For ease of work, do all the embroidery that you wish to do first, and add the wire at the end. If you are forming a bowl, it can help to put it into a bowl shape to dry, as it will retain more of the stiffening residue, although putting it over a form will work too. Ceramic or glass is best. I've also found that balloons, although they have the obvious advantage of being easily let down, seem to have a tendency to pull off some of the glue with them and the structure is then less firm. If you have included feet or decoration in metal on your bowl, it will be necessary to put it over something instead.

## RECYCLING WOOD WASTE

Wood seems to be fairly unexploited as an inclusion in embroidery and textile media, and yet the beauty of wood, bark and shavings, and their ability to add structure and texture to work, means that we should look at its possibilities.

### PENCIL SHAVINGS

Every time we get out our colouring pencils, pencil shavings abound, and as the wood around the pencil is often coloured this can create interesting pieces of coloured and natural wood. Try incorporating them into a sample by stitching over them or trapping them between layers of clear plastic before stitching.

Sticking them to threads or threads of glue can also be effective. On a Teflon sheet dribble interweaving strings of PVA glue; immediately before it dries, sprinkle over your saved pencil shavings. You may also incorporate bits of waste thread or small bits of fabric or paper.

## ATTACHING FINE WOOD

Wood can be attached to embroidery, or embroidery attached to wood, simply by wrapping and stitching or gluing with PVA. You might also consider drilling a series of small holes in the wood and stitching through it. Plan the holes so that the stitching that you intend doing will fit.

## FINE WOOD SHAVINGS

Fine wood shavings saved from a planer are ideal for incorporating into stitching as they can easily be hand stitched and integrated into the work. Alternatively, use PVA first and then stitch over and into them to integrate them.

They can be machine stitched on their own or into a surface. Wood shavings most often present a coiled form, which can be exploited to help mould a surface. Fine lace bowls, sculptures or jewellery can be made on vanishing fabric, with wood coils incorporated into the work for added structure as well as textural diversity.

*Above and below: Coloured pencil shavings arranged on a PVA structure on cellophane, then heated and stitched.*

*Above: Bowl made with wood shavings. The natural curve of the wood shavings was used to help form the bowl made with very lightweight stitching on Solusheet.*

*Below:* Bread Basket on Red-checked Tablecloth *by the author. Stitched by machine on a fine wooden packaging that some wholemeal bread came in. The plywood was split to be even finer.*

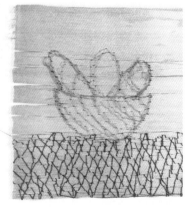

## STITCHING OVER OR INTO WOOD PIECES

Imagine wrapping and stitching on a large scale to incorporate sizeable pieces of wood. Consider suitable threads or string that will accept heavier weights. Incorporate cloth with looped seams to hold the wood into a structure. Sails, kites, wind-swept sea fences, mussel poles and fish netting can provide useful inspiration. Fine wood may be stitched into, or make appropriate holes instead.

### Ideas: bark

- Mulberry bark is a beautiful material and responds well to stitching, giving delicious textures to your work. It can be dyed or coloured easily with inks.
- The fine bark fibres from palm trees are actually a woven structure when pulled off the tree. You could work with the fibres in papermaking or fibre paper using wallpaper paste (see Chapter 1). You can also stitch directly onto the fibres by hand or machine.
- Cork can also be stitched by hand or machine if it is fine enough.
- Where bark is not thin enough to be stitched into, it can always be incorporated into work through couching, wrapping, gluing, or drilling with fine holes for hand stitching. If you can stitch by hand or machine into the surface, you can add the bark in other work to add surface texture that can be left natural or painted.

## BEACH COMBING

Washed-up, wave-beaten pieces of wood, coloured or not, carry their own history and jog our memories of beach holidays and the pleasures and peace of looking out to the open sea. Incorporating beach-combed pieces into textile work will add to the story that the embroidery will tell. Washed-up wood can also make interesting frames or poles for hangings.

## WOOD AND PAVAPOL FABRIC

Using wood as a structure for fabric sculpture through wrapping and using loops for seams may give fairly basic structures, but adding kites, sails or enclosures will make the resulting work more interesting. Try dipping the fabric in Pavapol before applying it to the wooden structure, or paint it thinly with Pavapol on both sides once the structure is created. One way to secure the wood while you are securing the structure with Pavapol-dipped fabric is to stick the wood pieces into a clay base while the sculpture is being formed.

*Above:* Small Beach *by the author. Worked on linen with acrylic, hand and machine stitching, stiff nylon after being used for cheat's paper, and a piece of driftwood for the hanging.*

*Above:* Sea Necklace *by Julieanne Long, made from stitched and bound stones and driftwood from beach combing expeditions.*

*Right: Palm tree vessel by the author. The fibres around a palm tree from the garden were interwoven in their natural state. They were then machine stitched, including a piece of wood bark, and then the structure stitched together by hand to make a vessel.*

*Below: Looped seam with inserted wood.*

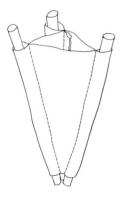

## USING MINERAL WASTES AND DEPOSITS IN TEXTILES

Working into natural materials and working natural materials into your work can give a sensation of space and calm to the piece. The notion of seascapes, rugged countryside or Japanese gardens that mineral inclusion can evoke, even if the work is completely abstract, allows the mind to wander into its own contemplations and meditations.

Some minerals can be included or added to the work by being drilled or holed and actually stitched into. Other pieces may have to be included with needle-made lace nets or machine-made laces stitched over them to hold them in position. Objects can be hung from textile pieces in the manner of beads through drilled holes or through the creation of a holding net structure.

## PEBBLES, STONES AND MINERAL GLASS

Pebbles or well-chosen stones can literally add weight to a piece, and even be used to weigh down a textile piece, or they can hang as 'beads' along an edge. Mineral glass can be found or bought in fine slivers, or use glass found on the beach, wave-washed smooth.

Sometimes such objects have natural holes in them and are just asking to be suspended. Otherwise, you will have to incorporate them using wrapping or lace techniques.

### Ideas

- Needlemade lace over pebbles can hold them to a surface, or could simply decorate the pebble entirely.
- A vanishing fabric lace could be made on the machine and then used over or round a pebble to support it or include it in the work.
- Consider wrapping pebbles or stones in wire before suspending them.
- Once hard objects are more or less enveloped in some way, they can then be suspended from work.

*Below:* Money Makes the World Go Round. *Shisha appliqué with some leftover Russian coins (donated by an Australian embroiderer on a visit). A very loose machine feather stitch was used. It's easier if you glue the pieces onto the fabric first. The fabric was leftover from the bottom of a curtain that was too long. The surface stitchery is with a thick rayon thread through a topstitch needle with a low top tension.*

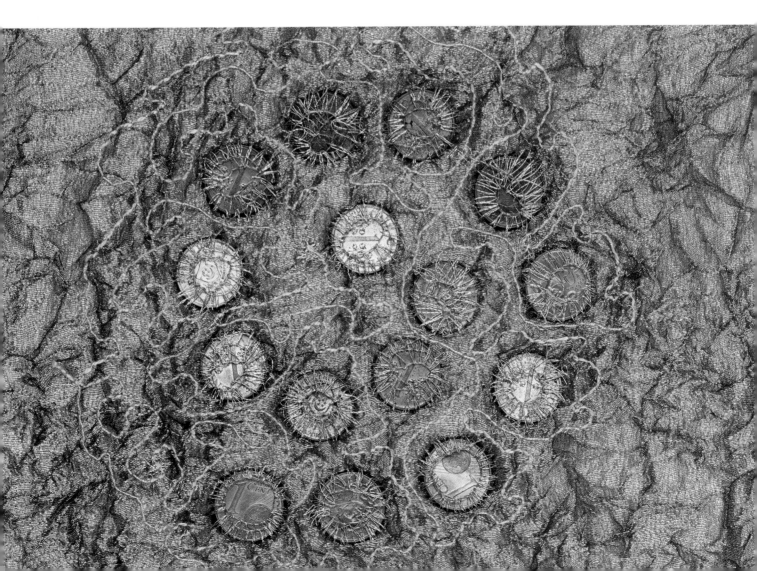

*Right: Drawing of needlemade lace and hand-stitched attachment.*

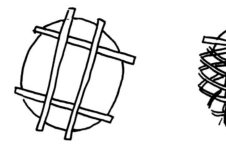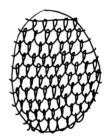

- Shisha glass application techniques can be useful for flatter stones, pebbles or glass. If they are very flat, you can use the most extreme feather stitch that your machine can make and stitch in circles around and around the outside of any flat object that is circular or ovoid in shape. Note that this can also work well for applying coins or flat buttons, or pieces of shell. It is easiest if you stick the object to the background first, then you only have to concentrate on the machining, and not on holding it at the same time. If you work slowly, you are less likely to break the needle if you hit the hard surface being applied, and you will also create a more extreme feather stitch. Hand stitching using shisha techniques can work well where the object is not flat enough or small enough to be applied by machine.
- A fine fabric, gauze, net, butter muslin or organdie could be placed over the pebbles and stitched around. Holes can be cut or burned into the fabric to allow the pebbles to show through more.

**Ideas: sand and shells**
- You may be lucky enough to find shells with holes in so that they can be stitched into embroidery; some shells accept drilling with a fine drill.
- Smaller objects such as sand or small shells can be imbedded into glue or acrylic paint surfaces for simple texture. Leave pathways in the glued-on sand to make machine stitching easier, or to make concentrated areas of texture.
- Shells or small particles of shells can be applied by stitching over them – consider shisha techniques (see above).
- Sand or fine shell pieces could be incorporated into varnish, PVA or Paverpol and used as a finishing coat for bowls or boxes.
- Sand and small pieces of shell can be incorporated into handmade paper, or silk or wool paper, made with wallpaper paste for added texture. (See chapters 1 and 4 for methods.)

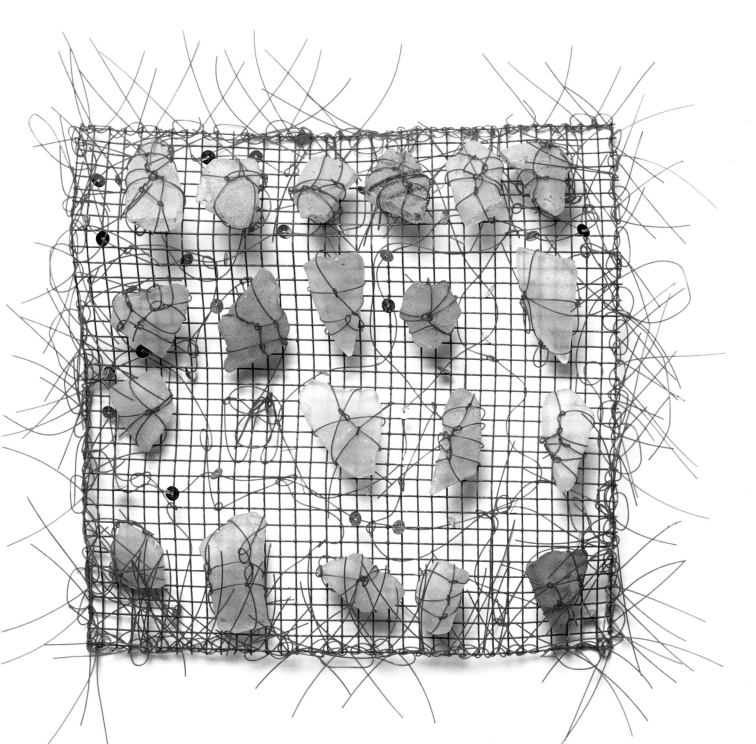

*Above: Julieanne Long: 'I had been looking at Indian textiles. I love bright colours and fabrics with shisha work on them. I wanted to do a piece based on this. The background is a piece of fencing mesh which I sprayed pink. Pieces of sea glass and sequins were added in a kind of needlelace stitch using pink fishing line. I then knotted this same fishing line around the edge.'*

*Above: Eau by the author. Sand is included in acrylic modelling medium to create texture. The whole is coloured with acrylic paint once dry. Stitches were included where the texture was lightest. The embroidery attached was worked on an embroidery machine with a Sfumato program from a photo of a boat call Rouseau du Lac. Just the EAU part was used as the work was about water.*

## EARTH COLOURS

The earth can provide us with many rich-coloured rocks. These can sometimes be crushed with a pestle and mortar and incorporated into acrylic wax, PVA or a fabric paint medium to add natural colours to your fabrics. Earth colours can be incorporated into hand-made papers for added colour and texture.

## FALSE STONE

For real stones, see page 87. For sculptural effects there is an additive for fabric hardener that resembles stone and can be added to give stone-like effects to your fabric sculptures. You can also add ground earth colours, sand or other minerals to acrylic medium or acrylic modelling paste, and paint onto this finish.

## SLATE

Old roofing slates can be fine and weathered. They may accept fine drilling with some difficulty, or otherwise they can be punched with a special tool to make holes suitable for stitching. You may have to ask a roofer (if you know one) if you can borrow such a tool! You can incorporate small pieces of slate into your textile work, using the same techniques as stones or pebbles. Slate has a wonderful solid, yet fragile appearance that tells the story of thousands of years of history in the ground, and of hundreds of years of history as a building material.

## CERAMICS

When you are making ceramic pieces from scratch to hold embroidered pieces, or to be incorporated into embroidery, it is possible to make holes in them at the 'green' stage before they are dried and fired. However, for recycled pieces of ceramics, this is not possible. Earthenware is less highly fired than other forms of pottery and you may find it possible to drill fine holes without losing too many pieces.

For applying bits of broken china to your embroidery, sand down the edges so that they are not sharp, and use the same methods as for incorporating pebbles and stones. Gluing the pieces first can help before you start to stitch. Try using a fine see-through fabric, such as gauze, butter muslin or net, placed over the sanded pieces and stitched around to hold the pieces down. Including bits of broken china in the work could be particularly emotive if you are trying to evoke a certain era or environment.

*Above Left:* Earth Colours, *worked on an artist's canvas and painted with metallic powders. The earth colours come from the south of France and have been ground with a pestle and mortar before being included in the acrylic medium. Hand stitching around the edge perhaps gives a notion of a patchwork or appliqué. Some of the mixed colours were also used for* Empty Shrine *(see page 42).*

*Above Right: Silk and wool paper made by Dany Pottier and including sand, bits of shell and pepper. The work was for a workbook sample based around the sea, hence the bird footprints in the sand.*

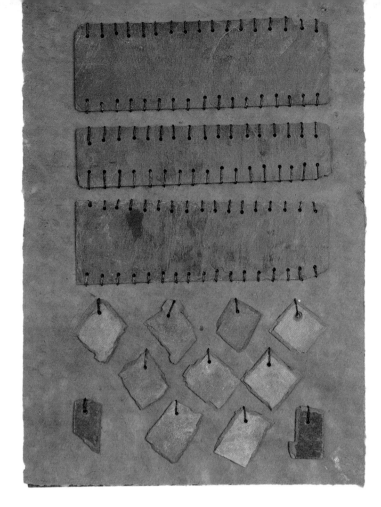

# COLLAGRAPHY

Collagraphy is an interesting way of using the textures of found objects to make printed images. It is a printing process that consists of making a plate or board for printing and adding texture to it, instead of working into the surface and taking things away, which is the basis of etching, woodblock or lino-printing.

The prepared collagraphic plate can be used to print on paper, handmade paper or even fabric. If you print on fabric or paper you can obviously stitch into it afterwards. For collagraphy, as with etching, it is preferable to use printing ink but, if this is out of the question, you could use oil paint. Cleaning the plate of oil paint or ink after printing can be difficult, so your print may be just a monotype (a one-off, as you throw away the plate after printing), or prints may not be identical if the plate gets damaged during cleaning. If this is not a problem, you may achieve several interesting, if not identical, prints. A rather unorthodox method, but one which works, is to re-ink the plate very quickly after printing an image, and continue printing further images, thus avoiding the sort of cleaning that could ruin the plate.

**You will need:**
- Strong cardboard or a fine wooden board (if this is textured it will add something to the final print. Don't use thick supports if you are able to use a press. PVC floor tiles can also offer a useful support – the non-shiny side will stick best, or sand the surface first. Flattened tin cans can be used for a support with epoxy resin glue.)

*Above: Hanging with slate. Hand stitching through slate and paper.*

*Opposite: Broken Heart with a Mirror of Vanity by the author. Worked with pieces of a broken cup. The cup was once part of a pair of his-and-hers cups until one was broken. Uses shisha techniques on an old skirt that has been discharged. The mirror is from an old garment belonging to my daughter, indicating other realities, past or future.*

- Different materials and textures to glue to this support, such as textured paper or cardboard, sand, different-textured fabrics, lace, embroidered surfaces, tins, masking tape, plants, leaves or flowers, any interesting object with a low relief, but note that plastics stick less well and should be sanded. (Note also that different objects will take on the ink or oil paint differently as they have different porosities; this could be exploited, but do be prepared for surprises. The ideal thickness is between 0.25–1 mm. Try not to go over 2–3 mm (¼ in). Green organic material resists better than dry, which is fragile and breaks easily, but green material sticks less well.)
- PVA medium, or synthetic resin glue, wood mastic or epoxy resin
- Gesso or matt acrylic medium
- Polyurethane varnish
- An etching or flower press or firm plastic inking roller
- Soft rubber mat for the press (or you can use the fine polystyrene foam that is sometimes used for protective wrapping)
- Printing inks or oil paint and linseed oil for dilution
- Short-cut stiff (cheap) brushes for inking or painting the plate
- Paper, which should be long grained
- Fabric – cotton and linen will give the best results (check on a sample that the ink seeps well into the surface of the fabric)
- Turpentine for cleaning

**Technique**

1. Seal the cardboard or thin wood with a coat of PVA on both sides and allow it to dry.
2. Arrange the objects and textures on the surface to obtain the desired effect.
3. Glue these objects and textures into place. One of the easiest and most comfortable glues to use is PVA (see other options above, but they will dry more quickly and are more unpleasant to use). Unfortunately PVA offers little resistance to the cleaning of the plate. This won't be a problem if you are planning to do monoprints, although the glue may cause the plate to stick to the wet paper during the printing process. If you wish to get more prints off your work, you can try protecting it with gesso or a polyurethane varnish. However, PVA may not always be suitable; if you are attaching things that are in relief or have spaces under them, it's best to apply them with wood mastic to fill in the gaps, so that they don't get squashed under the roller or press. Metal pieces such as wire staples, paper clips and so on are best applied with epoxy resin as they stick badly with other glues. Don't use too much glue when sticking fabrics or you will lose the textural quality.
4. Once your plate is textured and the elements are all glued into place, allow it to dry, then paint with two coats of gesso over the surface. Allow it to dry between coats.
5. Add two coats of varnish if you wish to further protect your plate.

6.  Now test the pressure of your press or of your own pressure with the roller: put a piece of paper to soak for about 30 minutes so that it becomes supple, but wring it out with the roller or by passing it through the press between two pieces of felt before you use it. If you are to use a roller, place the rubber mousse on a surface, followed by the paper (it may help to put a piece of felt between the mousse and the paper), then the plate without ink, and test with a roller. You will see when the pressure is right as there will be an even imprint on the paper. Working with a roller is a little more delicate, so you can adjust the way you present the plate and soft support and the paper to find out what is best for your particular plate.

7.  If you are able to use a press, place the plate (without ink) on the base of the press, followed by the damp paper, then a piece of felt or the rubber mat if the textures are particularly heavy. Press firstly with a light pressure, then increase the pressure until you achieve a good result with all the textures showing up on the paper.

8.  You can now ink or paint the plate. The ink or paint should not be too stiff or it will be difficult for it to enter the textures. If you have to thin it, don't over do it, and mix well. As you are going to paint the ink or paint onto the plate, you will be able to use several colours and place them as you wish, although they may blend during printing, so be careful about your colour

*Below Left: Plate with bits and pieces of fabric corrugated cardboard, and onion netting, with two coats of gesso ready for printing.*

*Below Centre: Resulting print on fine cotton fabric.*

*Below Right: Resulting print on paper.*

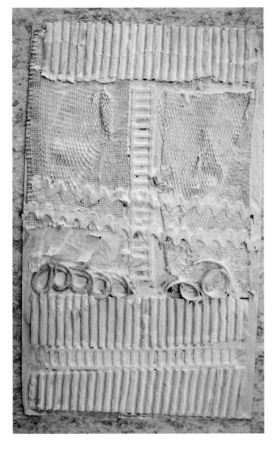
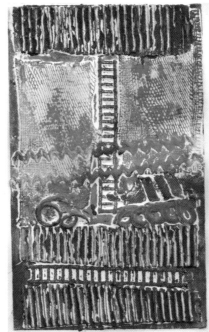

choice. If the plate isn't too overloaded with texture, you could try rolling the ink onto the plate. You will need to remove excess ink from the plate with cloths that are not too absorbent – nylon or acrylic. Use one that will be dirty to take off the excess ink, and one that will be clean to remove any remaining ink; try to push it further into the nooks and crannies of the textures. Wipe the edges of the plate, so that you don't get ink marks. You may wish to take the ink off certain surfaces for a better result.

9. Once the plate is inked, it must be printed immediately, as some of the incorporated objects or areas could be more absorbent than others, despite all of the precautions. Work as before, using the pressures that you have established.

10. When removing the paper from the plate, you must take very special care as it will have had to mould itself into the form of the plate, and will be very fragile. If you tear it, perhaps you could stitch it back together!

11. Paper can be piled up between layers of felt to dry if you do more than one print, or left on a flat surface – but it can curl up if not flattened. If you place it between layers of felt, put a piece of tissue paper on the ink side.

12. Clean the plate with rags, using white spirit. Use a paintbrush or old toothbrush in difficult areas. You can re-ink the plate and use it again immediately. Be careful not to overcharge areas with ink.

*Left:* The World is Your Oyster*; fusible synthetic fibres encased a real oyster shell with pearls (not real ones) in the bottom of the oyster shell.*

96

## Ideas

- Instead of using paper you can use a fabric, in which case you won't need to wet it because it is already supple enough.
- The resulting prints on fabric or paper could be embroidered, or have real bits and pieces incorporated into them.

As a conclusion to this chapter I think the most important thing to say is that the world is your oyster – you simply have to explore and keep your eyes open to find new ideas.

*Above: Strip patchwork with tarlatan left over from the collagraphy and etching process. Tarlatan is used to wipe the etching plate.*

97

# CHAPTER SEVEN
# RECYCLING BOOKS
# AND PACKAGING

Recycling papers and packaging, images and everyday finds into something meaningful or fun, with cultural references or memories is a valid art practice, if often a very personal one. The inclusion of important found objects within textile or embroidered surfaces may jog the memories of other people who have also had that experience or who can relate to it in some way.

Recycling existing packaging in the form of boxes can be as painstaking as making your own from scratch if a perfect finish is to be achieved, but you may also choose this method of re-appropriation to make a comment on packaging – in such a case a re-used look may be as appropriate as anything.

*Right: Recycled* Mother's Letters*, part of a 'reliquary series' by Mary Crehan.*

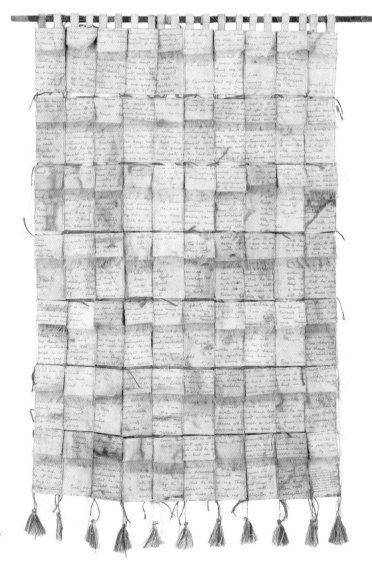

Altering books is becoming an art form in its own right, and so much has already been written on the subject, very often of the more painterly kind or the cut-and-stick variety, that there is very little to add in technical terms. However, it is such an important phenomena that it's worth addressing.

# WORKING WITH BOOKS

Books and printed paper can be a very useful starting point for any kind of art work. The very use of a complicated surface that may literally have a story to tell in its own right can be a very strong statement. It's worth considering books as a starting point for a textile artist or embroiderer, who will approach the book with stitches and fabric more so than with paint and glue.

### PRACTICALITIES

Working with hand stitches, fabrics, appliqué, and painting or dyeing is possible within the confines of a book without having to take it apart, or addressing the work simply to pages. However, machine stitching becomes a little more complicated unless you choose a book that can easily be bent out of the way giving access to one page at a time – even so movement will be restricted. For this reason it may be preferable to deconstruct the book and either present the pages separately or reconstruct the book after the embroidery has taken place, either as the book once again, or in a different format. Machine embroidery could be more simply included if worked onto separate fabrics of vanishing fabric that can then be incorporated with gluing or hand stitching.

### DECONSTRUCTION

This could take on the appearance of a smaller handmade book; a patchwork; a concertina of pages; individual pages treated with care and presented as images in their own right; pages could be cut out of the book, treated with machine embroidery and textile work and then be stitched in or glued to other pages that have been left in the book. Vanishing fabric or other machine techniques can be created and applied to pages that are left within a book. The book can be carefully deconstructed, worked into, then reconstructed as a book once the work is finished.

*Below: One of thirteen pages stitched from* Les Métamorphoses de Ovide. *This one is called* Du Désordre des Lectures. *Worked by Fanny Violet on transparent vinyl. The image works from both sides and the book was reformed.*

## CHOICE OF BOOK

The choice of book is, I feel, important. The title of the book or its content can be used to give an impetus to what you are trying to say through using it, although some people may feel that leaving this aspect to chance is an art statement in itself! In any case do be aware of copyright matters. You may use any book you wish as an altered book as a one-off art statement but, if you are planning to publish the work, you must make sure that it's out of copyright before choosing a particular book. See page 120 for more details on this issue.

It's important to consider the content of the book and the visual impact of the pages, whether they are illustrated or are just the written word. Many altered books make use of the written word to underline a new message by highlighting some words, or effacing others. Embroidery can obviously be used to this end.

*Right and opposite:* Good Housekeeping *by the author. Selected pages from* Mrs Beaton's book of Household Management *dictate how to be a woman and run a home. The frame for the bodice, made of cardboard with paper clips and instructions for changing the size, was made by Good Housekeeping and was for home dressmaking (for our perfect housekeeper). It probably dates from just after World War II. I found it in a flea market in France, though it's written on in German and American. It's easy to laugh at this kind of inculcation of the feminine ideal, but books on becoming a 'domestic goddess' are still being written and printed*

# CHAPTER XXVIII.

## GENERAL OBSERVATIONS ON CREAMS, JELLIES, SOUFFLES, OMELETS, & SWEET DISHES.

1385. CREAMS.—The yellowish-white, opaque fluid, smooth and unct to the touch, which separates itself from new milk, and forms a layer at its surface, when removed by skimming, is employed in a variety of culinary preparations. The analyses of the contents of cream have been decided to be, in 100 parts—butter 3.5; curd

*Above: A book cover by Fanny Violet, with Paris metro map and embroidery.*

## IMAGES

Images could be added to the book to underline or re-enforce the message or the story. If there are images already in the book, they could be underlined or reproduced with stitching or appliqué. A book that is concerned with a tourist venue, or a collection of maps, can be highlighted with real images or collections of paraphernalia collected during your own visit. Embroidered images or printing on fabric and inclusion within the pages can also be useful. (For methods of fabric printing from photographic images discussed see page 110). If you are separating pages from the book, you can photocopy other images onto them, leaving the words showing through. If the book is staying intact, try printing onto very fine fabrics and stitching them in, or print onto, adhesive webbing; iron these images directly onto the page. The result could be quite old and used.

## STITCHING

When paper is overstitched, it tends to deteriorate, a fact that can be used to advantage. If you don't want heavily stitched paper to fall apart, it can be backed. Fine *habutai* silk backing will not ruin the feel of the paper but will stop the paper falling to bits. Butter muslin may be useful for holding scraps of paper together, creating a used feel to the work.

If paper is stitched with large straight stitches it will hold together perfectly well, so creating patchwork from an existing book, or re-stitching worked pages together to form a smaller book or concertina is a real possibility.

If you want your book to look older and more used than it is, you could try singeing the edges (have water in a spray or a bowl of water handy), or dye the pages with left-over tea.

*Below:* Le Bikini Rouge de Margot *by Fanny Violet. Made from the every day French postage stamp (a bikini the size of a postage stamp) and the post marks. The stitching is very close together with a shaded red thread.*

## CARDBOARD BOOK

A child's cardboard book is a useful starting point for a series of embroideries requiring window mounts. With matching window mounts cut into two consecutive pages, these could be glued together to sandwich an embroidery or image that works from both sides, or you could place two embroideries back to back. A child's embroidery can be presented in this way, perhaps retelling the story told in the book.

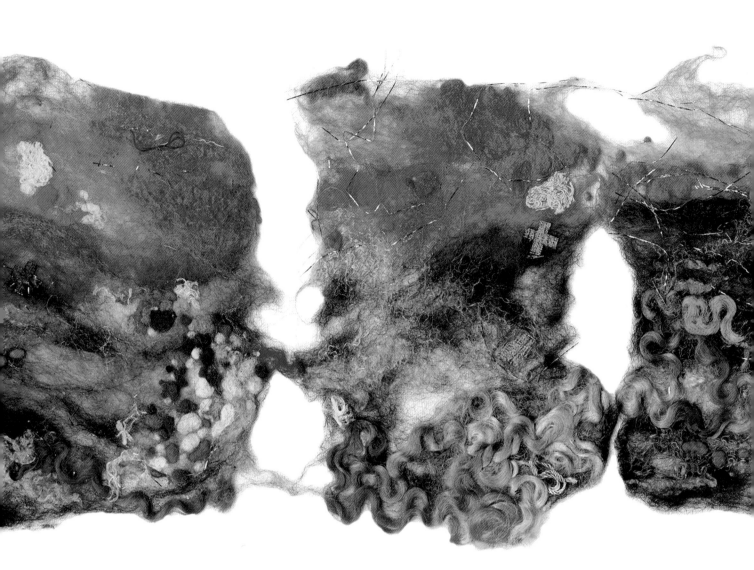

**PROJECT: CONCERTINA BOOKS**

**Technique**

1. With pages taken from your chosen book, work on them to create something new with adjusted or reinforced images and meanings. Dyeing, hand or machine stitching, adding bits of pieces of fabric, images, printing, lace, paint, lace, buttons, beads, paper clips, bus tickets, recipes, remarks, whatever is appropriate to the book or what you are trying to say.

2. You may need to varnish the pages once you have worked them: clear acrylic varnish is available in matt or shiny, brush-on or spray, to help homogenise a surface.

3. Stitch the edges of the pages together with a large zigzag stitch, binding tape or ribbon, so that the book can be easily folded without damage; make sure that, when the book is opened from its concertina form, the pages run one after another in order. You can let the continuation happen on the back of the pages.

4. Make covers and a spine if you wish the book to be closed and presented as such, and glue or stitch the back of the last page to the back cover.

## PROJECT: SIMPLE CLOTH BOOKS

Making a simple cloth book out of scraps of fabric or linen sheet can give a useful starting point for an unusual embroidery sketchbook.

1. Decide on the size you wish your book to be and cut out pages this size. You can edge the pages with satin-stitched or over-lock (serged) edges to prevent them from fraying.
2. Stitch down one side of the book to hold all the pages together. If you want to include lots of pages or want to be able to keep adding pages, or changing the order, you can make a row of eyelets or buttonholes along one edge and lace the book together.

Another method is to cut the fabric twice the size of the pages required (width-wise), and stitch them down the middle (neaten the edges first, if preferred). Now you can fold the book to make a simple exercise book. The book can become thicker, by making another exercise book the same and stitching them together by using a spine along the stitched edge. A firm piece

*Above:* Loose Connections *by Mary-Clare Buckle. The artwork is in the form of a continuous folding 'book' of six square pages. The pages were allowed to attach themselves to each other during the felting process.*

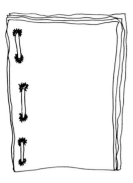

*Above: Pages held together with eyelets and cord.*

*Right: Making a book with kebab sticks for the spine. Four individual exercise books were made and stitched together down the centre, the books were then folded in half. A kebab stick was added along each folded edge with a wide zigzag stitch. The kebab sticks were then stitched together by hand, just as in book binding.*

of something (a kebab stick for example) can be stitched along the edge of the spine of each book. This could quite easily be added with a zigzag stitch or included in a seamed binding. These individual spines are then stitched together after placing the 'exercise' books exactly one on top of the other. There are traditional ways to do this, but with a little imagination you will come up with your own interweaving decorative stitching to hold your spines together!

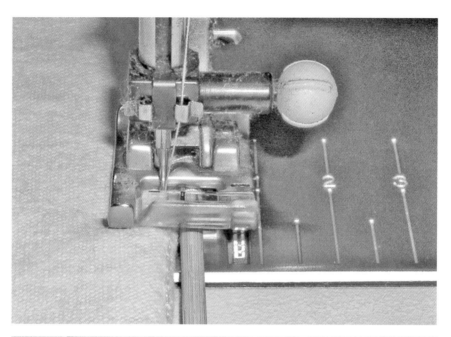

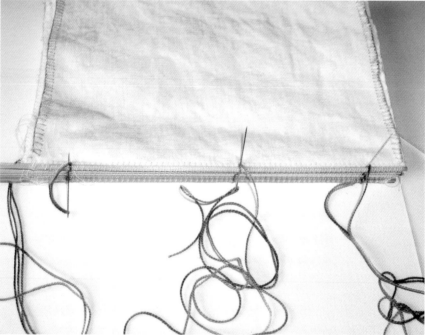

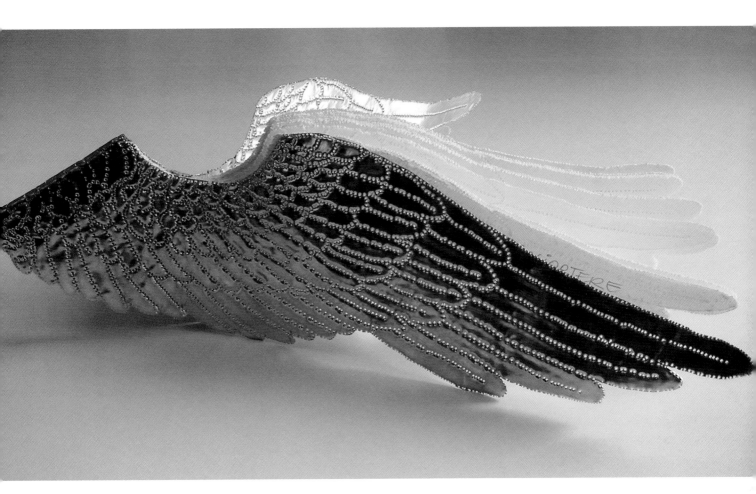

*Above: Worked on recycled
wine bottle topping in stitch
marks only by Fanny Violet.*

*Below:* Miniature Garden *by the author. The box was a chocolate box, painted with gesso and covered with vanishing fabric and silk throwster's waste. The 'seed packets' inside are made with silk throwster's waste and invisible thread on dissolvable Solusheet. Seeds have been gathered from the garden we made in our old house and included in each seed packet. Thus I can keep my garden in miniature.*

## MAKING EMBROIDERED BOXES USING EXISTING BOXES FROM PURCHASED GOODS

I have less than fond memories of making correct cardboard-formed boxes, and yet the notion of an enclosed boxed space is so intriguing that it begs attention.

### USING BOXES AS CONTAINERS FOR SPECIAL OBJECTS

Boxes can be a useful starting point to assemble a collection of objects that you wish to bring attention to, as an art statement, a collection of memories or as all three at once.

**Ideas**

- Covering boxes with glued fabric and varnish or PVA for firmness and durability.
- Covering boxes with machine-embroidered fabric made on dissolvable fabric such as Romeo or Solusheet for firmness. PVA varnish or Paverpol can be added for extra firmness.
- Seaming together fabric to cover the sides of the box, covering inside and outside. The bottom inside and out could be covered card glued into place.

*Below: Caskets by Maria Walker. Scraps of fabric and threads were trapped between layers of cling film then each layer was bonded using an iron. The caskets were machined all over using vermicelli stitch, rubbed with metallic wax and decorated with handmade cords and beads. The smaller casket uses strips of old coloured carrier bags and fabrics, woven and bonded together using a hot iron.*

# CHAPTER EIGHT
# RECYCLING IMAGES

## INCORPORATING PRINTED IMAGES AND THE PRINTED WORD INTO EMBROIDERY

Recycling real found or collected images or the printed word into your embroidery and textile images can be useful to make statements or to retain memory. We find more and more borrowed images and words as part of contemporary art practice, and this can certainly have a place in embroidery and textile art. Souvenirs from your own or your families' lives can be incorporated into textiles as a memory piece about people or places.

There are many ways of incorporating found images or words into your work that will leave the image or words apparent or obliterate them, leaving only a vague trace. For choices about how to incorporate them and what method to use, you can experiment with the following techniques. I have included a section on interpreting current copyright law in relation to this.

## TRANSFERRING IMAGES TO TEXTILES

There are many ways of transferring photographic images to textile surfaces; here are some of the easiest and safest. These methods work variously with home inkjet printers, photocopiers and newspaper (the cheaper kind – not glossy magazines).

### ADHESIVE WEBBING TRANSFERS

Adhesive webbing such as Bondaweb have long been used by embroiderers to transfer paint, ink and other coloured mediums onto fabrics in an interesting and easy way. You can also use this method for printed images.

This is a method using your own home printer, mainly because many people are far too scared to put foreign objects through their printers, and may prefer you not to use theirs! I assume that there would be a problem with putting the adhesive webbing through the heat of a photocopier, although some brands produce less heat, but I haven't dared ask any commercial photocopier to try. However, I have found that adhesive webbing or Bondaweb goes through my home printer rather easily while still attached to its backing paper (obviously). I have even found that I don't have to clean the heads afterwards – which isn't always true with other foreign objects such as silk paper and other odd papers and fabrics, but you might prefer to do so.

**Technique**

1. Select your image. If you have a printer that's also a photocopier you can photocopy something directly onto the adhesive webbing. But it's better to scan the image into your computer so that you can play with it, or use one of your own digital photographs. You will need to reverse or flip the image in your computer because, if you don't, the image will come out the wrong way round once ironed onto the fabric.

   If you have a program on your computer such as Photoshop or Paintshop Pro, open the chosen image and just enhance the colours a little (saturation), as this will put more colour onto the adhesive webbing – there is always some loss in the image when ironing on. Don't overdo it or you will change the colours entirely.

   You may also wish to crop the image to choose the exact bit you want to use, and adapt the size of the image chosen to fit the printer or to fit your intended use. Of course you can play further with the image on your computer programs if you wish to.

2. Once you are happy with your image, you can print it onto your adhesive webbing, placed carefully into the feeder of your printer. I always ask the computer to show a preview of the printed image if I'm not sure about the size.

3. Print it off.

4. You can now iron the image with the webbing face down onto your fabric. A fine grained material such as *habutai* silk will give the best results, but I've also experimented with close-grained fine cotton scrims, which are fun to stitch on.

5. Allow the work to cool slightly before pulling off the paper backing.

6. Now you can stitch on and work into the image as much or as little as you wish to.

*Above: Photo image printed onto adhesive webbing and then onto silk.*

*Above: This image has been photocopied directly onto fabric.*

## TRANSFERS WITH CITRUS SOLVENT

Citrus solvent is available in various concentrations (choose the strongest you can) and is an industrial cleaning agent, used most notably against graffiti. It's made from lemon and orange skin and is safer environmentally than chemical solvents. It is a little greasy and needs careful attention if the result is not to run or smear.

This method requires an ink base that uses toner and so will not work with laser photocopiers. It will work with black photocopies, colour photocopies (get them done on cheap paper) and some magazines and newspapers – the cheaper ones.

If you are using black and white photocopies, go for high contrast, and avoid too much grey. On colour photocopies, the colours that transfer are not always as subtle as on the original, so be prepared for this. Glossy magazines won't work.

**You will need:**

- Pre-washed fabric; silk can give well defined images, but it's up to you to experiment
- Soft absorbent fabric, folded to place under your fabric for printing. This will absorb excess solvent and help prevent the image from being blurred
- A photocopy – try first with a black and white one. Then you can experiment with colour images and magazines. If there is lettering, do remember to copy the work backwards first or your lettering will be back to front. Make a transparent copy first or flip the image over on your computer before printing, then photocopy the reversed image
- Rubber gloves
- Citrus solvent
- A plant mister, or similar sprayer, or a firm sponge
- Old plastic or wooden spoon that you won't use again for cooking, or a rubber printing roller

### Technique

1. Place your fabric on the pile of absorbent cloth and place the photocopy ink side down on top.
2. With the solvent in the sprayer, spray the photocopy until you can see the image through to the back; sponge the back, firmly pressing it onto the fabric underneath. With either method you will need to practise to get used to how much solvent to use.
3. Holding the copy in place to prevent it from smearing, rub firmly on the back of the paper with a spoon, or roll the roller very firmly over it.
4. Carefully peel up a corner of the image to see how things are going. If it is not transferring well enough, you haven't used enough solvent, so spray a little more in those areas that need it.
5. Gently peel the photocopy off the fabric and dispose of it safely. You do not need heat to set the ink onto the fabric. Remove the printed image

carefully until it is thoroughly dry, as the image can easily smear when wet.

6. You can now include the images in any of your work; stitch them, add colour with fabric paints, or dyes and so on. The main interest of this technique, I feel, is the use of newspaper print as a subject and the used quality of the effect you get.

## ACRYLIC GEL MEDIUM TRANSFER

Acrylic gel medium (gloss) is used to build up surfaces in acrylic painting, and is available in various textures and thickness. For this experiment, you simply need a smooth glossy or soft gloss gel. If you don't like the shiny result once finished, matt gels or varnishes are available. The problem with gel transfer is that the resulting fabric does have the dressing on it, so it might not be what you're looking for.

### Technique 1

1. Paint your photocopied or printed image with a layer of gel.
2. Paint the area of the fabric with gel where the image is to be printed.
3. Allow the gel to dry completely. Once dry use a medium hot iron protected with baking parchment, and iron the image onto the prepared fabric.
4. Peel off the paper once the image has cooled. If it is stubborn, you can use a soft damp towel to remove it. However, do be careful, especially if you have used an image produced on an inkjet printer – this ink is water soluble, so you could lose part of the image if you rub too hard or get it too wet. You shouldn't encounter this problem with a photocopied image.

*Below:* Interlude *by Pascale Doire. Surface created with ink from magazines and publicity leaflets using trichloroethylene. This technique is creative but it has its constraints and limits. You can create a new surface with the superposition of inks, graphic effects and images which can be composed ready for embroidery, painting or quilting. However, precautions must be taken with all solvents so as not to breathe in the vapours of the trichloroethylene. The magazines need to have been produced cheaply, if the ink is of good quality the solvent won't dissolve the ink. Another limitation is that it's difficult to obtain saturated colours using this method, but this can be part of its charm.*

**Technique 2**

This does not work with inkjet printer images as the work is too wet after printing, but you will be able to use photocopies and cheap magazines or newspapers.

1. Coat the image with the gel and immediately place face down on the fabric.
2. Using a roller or the back of a spoon, rub or roll over the surface firmly so that the gel adheres to the fabric.
3. Turn the image and fabric over and roll or rub again.
4. Allow the gel to dry fully, overnight if necessary, then soak in water for about 10 minutes to allow the paper to soften.
5. Very patiently pull and rub the paper away.
6. Allow to dry fully.
7. You can colour the gel medium image with any colouring material.

## DYLON IMAGE MAKER

Dylon Image Maker works with photocopied images in the same way as acrylic gel. The pack comes complete with instructions.

## LAZERTRAN TRANSFER

Lazertran is a relatively widely available slide paper transfer medium. There are several Lazertran papers which are suitable for many different surfaces. For our purposes we will look at Lazertran silk paper, and Lazertran textile inkjet paper, which is available for light or dark fabrics.

### Technique 1: Lazertran silk paper

This product is designed to be used with toner-based printers on closely woven silk or satin or on other fabrics that have been treated first. The resulting fabrics are flexible and retain their draping qualities.

For transferring onto open weave or other fabrics than silk, spray 3M permanent Photo Mount Spray over the fabric first and allow it to dry. You can now use this fabric as follows:

1. Copy your image in reverse onto a sheet of Lazertran silk.
2. On Pre-washed and ironed fabric, place the paper over the fabric face down.
3. Iron with a hot iron until it is stuck, being careful not to touch the image with the iron.
4. Immerse the silk in water and leave until the backing paper comes off on its own.
5. Remove the silk carefully from the water and iron with a cool iron face down until dry.
6. Turn over, and with baking parchment between the iron and the image, iron with a hot iron; allow it to cool before peeling off the baking parchment.
7. If the image is shiny and seems to be sitting on the surface of the fabric, it is best to redo step 6 to push the image into the fibres.

**Technique 2: Lazertran textile inkjet paper**

This can be used on all textile surfaces and is very simple, but the result is harder and less suitable for stitching.

1.  Print the image in reverse on an inkjet printer.
2.  With a hot iron, iron the Lazertran face down onto a Pre-washed and ironed fabric.
3.  When it is cool, you can carefully peel the backing paper away.

# PHOTOCOPYING OR PRINTING ON TEXTILES

### PRINTING DIRECTLY ONTO FABRIC

You can place any paper and any fabric you dare into your home printer and print your image onto it. Printing onto weird and wonderful surfaces can be quite expensive in printing ink, especially as you may have to clean the heads afterwards, but you can print onto cotton, silk, canvas, linen, handmade papers (within reason!), silk paper and so on. If your printer has good photo quality ink, the result will actually be fast for occasional delicate washing.

**Technique**

1.  Iron fabrics onto freezer paper, or attach them with spray glue or double-sided tape to a thin card surface. The fabric must be attached perfectly to its support if it is to pass through the printer without any problems. Fabrics should not be too thick or too textured so that they pass easily through your printer, but common sense and experience will be your guide. One useful way with any fabric is to iron it to an adhesive webbing such as

*Below:* Secret Garden *by Yvonne. The inspiration for the embroidery was taken from a series of photographs taken in the gardens of Belton House, a National Trust Property in Lincolnshire, UK. The central image has been printed from one of the original photographs on a fine cotton lawn using the Bubble jet 2000 system. The image has then been set within a frame of handmade cotton wool paper dyed with procion dyes. Machine-wrapped cords have been couched to the surface and further surface texture has been achieved with machine embroidery on cold water dissolvable fabric. The piece has been completed with hand embroidery and beading.*

Bondaweb, leaving the backing paper attached for firmness, and then put this through the printer.

2. Print your desired image onto the fabric.
3. If you have used the adhesive webbing method above, with patience or heat you will be able to pull the webbing off the back of the fabric, or you will be able to use this adhesive webbing to bond or appliqué your image to another surface.
4. If the heads touch the surface of the fabric or paper, you may need to clean the heads after printing.

## PRINTING ONTO PRE-PREPARED FABRIC

Prepared fabric can be bought in prepared sizes for your printer, or in rolls. If you are concerned about the quality of the ink in your printer and its ability to resist light and washing, you may prefer to use printer-prepared fabric.

### Technique

Less expensive than buying pre-prepared fabric and also less expensive than transfer papers is a product called Bubble Jet 2000. Although printing done with this product will fade eventually, the result is much more fast than when printing on untreated fabric, so it would be useful if you're planning to create something that will need regular washing, such as a quilt or garment.

**You will need:**
- Rubber gloves
- Bubble Jet 2000
- A deep tray for the soaking (the one you used for your papermaking!)
- Fabric (cut to the size of your printer), pre-washed and ironed can work better, 100% cotton or silk for best results
- Towel
- Iron
- Freezer Paper
- Your image

**Note:** You are advised to work in a well ventilated environment and use rubber gloves.

1. Shake the bottle of Bubble Jet 2000 and pour about 2 cm (¾ in) into the tray. In a 960 ml (33¾ fl oz) bottle you will have enough for 50–60 sheets of fabric. You can put left-over product back into the bottle and reuse it.
2. Allow each sheet of fabric to soak for 5 minutes, then take it out and dry flat on a towel. At this point the fabric will be a little stiff.

*Left:* Mona Lisa *by the author. Machine embroidery on noile silk.*

3.  Once dry, iron the fabric to freezer paper and print out your image onto the fabric, then leave it for 30 minutes.
4.  You can then machine wash it with a delicate detergent to fix it, or hand wash using the bubble jet rinse. Agitate for 3 minutes.
5.  Once dry the fabric will be back to its normal draping qualities.

The best results seem to be obtained by using fabric that has just been treated, although you could try storing it in an air-free environment to maintain this quality. The treated fabrics retain more of the ink from the printer than non-treated fabrics, and will stand more washing and wear, if this is an important issue.

## EMBROIDERY TRANSFER

Sometimes a simply drawn outline can say a lot, especially for a well-known image or face. If there are problems with the copyright of the image you have chosen, a simple line drawing done by yourself (even if traced from an image) should not attract adverse attention.

Many artists have done their version of the Mona Lisa. To transfer the image for my version, I simply traced the lines I considered to be important onto a lightweight tracing paper or tissue paper. (The sort of paper that is used to wrap shirts is ideal if you are looking to recycle!) The tracing paper was then attached to the silk noile I used for the embroidery, and I used free-motion stitching through both layers with medium length stitches to trace this outline into place. I used the thread that was going to be the final choice, in this case gold. However, you can use this method to transfer an image using the same colour thread as the background, or a dissolvable thread, and afterwards stitch in the colours you wish to use.

The background of the Mona Lisa was added afterwards. The original painting was kept by Napoleon in his bathroom, which is where mine has her place!

## USING AN EMBROIDERY MACHINE

With the increased use of photography in art and as an art tool, particularly computer-adjusted photographs, it seems normal that the inclusion of photographic images should reach embroidery and textile art. I have discussed methods of printing images, including photographic ones, directly onto your fabric to be used, embroidered, or left untouched as you think fit.

Another approach is to embroider the photographic image itself. Computer programs available for computerised embroidery machines allow for very good photographic reproduction using the Sfumato technique of layering different colours. This usually employs a sort of vermicelli as the embroidery stitch, and, as this stitch bears a close relation to free-motion stitching, it's quite easy to include such embroidery machine images within the context of your own embroidery. So just as we often see photos included into other art work with layers of paint or other mixed media, an embroidered photo or image can be recycled into your embroidery and further embellished. You can use paints or stitching, or the image could be stitched onto fabric that is already pre-prepared and treated with dyes, paints, bronzing powders or appliqué, before being stitched.

If you have access to an embroidery machine and program try the following:
1.  Take a photo that interests you and ask your embroidery program to reproduce it in black and white. You can play with the contrasts in the program or beforehand in your photo program. Save.
2.  Ask the program to do the same but in colour. Accentuating the saturation of the image can be interesting.
3.  See how much you can simplify the essential shapes or obscure the details of the image by using extreme contrasts, extreme saturation and other filters available on your photo program, and try them out in the embroidery program.
4.  Compare the results between very life-like photos and the gradual loss of the image.

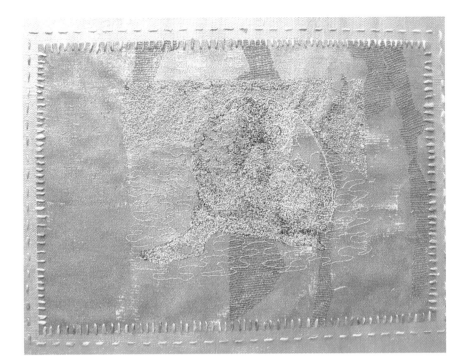

### Ideas

- Experiment with embroidering the image on ordinary white cotton or fabric that has been dyed in an interesting way, or otherwise coloured – perhaps with bronzing powders or coloured adhesive webbing.
- Try making a simple seamed patchwork and using this as a background – strong coloured stripes will affect how the image can be perceived.
- Try working on net as a background – lighten the stitch density. You can support net with a fine Aquafilm backing.
- Try working on paper – you could place it on an Aquafilm or muslin Heataway backing or on fine silk, then Aquafilm. The one will give more support than the other once the stitching is finished.
- Once it has been worked, try stitching with your embroidery – highlighting or outlining areas for more definition.
- Try applying paint or bits of fabric, fibres or gauze over areas and stitching around the image and 'accidentally' into it to gradually destroy it or hide or obscure the image.

### SKETCHBOOK AND PAPER WORK

Sketchbook and paper work are always important and learning how to incorporate real images, hijacked, borrowed and otherwise recycled from the real world is no different. Such images have a valid place in contemporary art practice, but need to be part of the initial concept and really included into the work if the result is to be successful. Practising incorporating real images in your sketchbook with crayons, pastels, paper collage and paint will help you to understand how you can make this work for you. When doing this, I have found it best to work with photographic images printed on ordinary paper or art paper, rather than shiny photographs, which are much more difficult to integrate into a surface. Such preparatory paper work can help to indicate how techniques of stitching, dying or patching can be used to the best advantage, so that the inclusion of such images is total and not just an add on.

# COPYRIGHT MATTERS

Does copyright matter? For your art statement you will need to consider the best way of incorporating the desired image or words, but you may also need to consider copyright law. Although the law can be a bit foggy about borrowed images and words in art production, I have included various pointers to help with issues relating to using borrowed images, words and books in your work.

### WHAT IS A COPYRIGHT?

The notion of copyright derives directly from The Statute of Anne in 1710 when a previous exclusive publishing act was overturned and authors were given exclusive rights to publish their work for 14 years, renewable for 14 years if they were still alive. The French also claim to have invented copyright law before this.

A copyright is a form of intellectual property that grants its holder the sole legal right to copy the works of 'original expression', such as literary works, film, music, sound recording, painting, computer programs or industrial design, and this for a given period of time.

### THE TIME FACTOR

For literary, dramatic, musical, artistic work or computer programs, the duration of the copyright is for 70 years after the last remaining author has died, or after it has been made available to the public; for sound recordings it is 50 years, and for film 70 years. The typographical arrangement of published editions is 25 years from first publication.

### THE PUBLIC DOMAIN

When an artist has been dead for more than 70 years, his or her work is in the public domain. Reproduction rights are then in the hands of those who have made reproductions of the work – for example the postcards made by the museum holding the work. In theory, if you took a snapshot of the work, you could do whatever you liked with it, but where museums have signs everywhere telling you that you cannot take photos, such a photo could not be used for reproductive purposes without the museum's permission, and this often includes a payment. Art, including art works, however, would cause less problems than reproduction and should be acceptable. It's best to follow this notion, as owners of such work can claim that a reproduction of the property that they hold is an infringement on their rights, and demand compensation for use, if they can prove that you have deliberately caused them financial or other hardship – which would be true if you were reproducing and selling an image that they also had been selling as postcards because they owned it. The more well-known and widely available an image is, the more difficult it is for a museum to claim 'ownership' of that image, so let that be your guide. Any photograph that you take of any work of art where the author has been dead for more than 70 years, can be used by yourself for your own purposes.

Above: Sketchbook work to incorporate real images. Drawings recalling the ice rink outside the Marie, the trees with fairy lights and snow outside La Grande Palace (and everywhere else) have been added to a photocopied map of Paris. Ticket entrance to the Pompedou centre, metro tickets and the top from a Champagne bottle have also been added.

If you take a picture of a field, garden or house and use that in your embroidery, it cannot be considered that you are causing prejudice; although asking the owner's permission isn't necessary, it can sometimes be polite if the reproduction is very personal and not so obviously in the public domain. Other buildings, less personal, are quite obviously in the public domain – all the chateaux you can visit and photograph, the streets of Venice, the sites of London and the details of all such things. If the building is not obviously in the public domain, for instance where the architect is still alive or only recently died, then the arguments will be related to 'fair use'.

### WHAT ABOUT WHEN THE OBJECT IS STILL UNDER COPYRIGHT?

We come here to fair use! This is really shaky ground, but, basically, if you're using something still under copyright in a non-substantial way and making a one-off piece of art out of it, you should be able to use it.

The judgements used about whether something is for fair use are the following:
- **The purpose and character of the use,** including whether the use of the object was for reproduction of the object as it stood and was for personal profit, or whether the reproduction was for educational purposes.

121

- **The nature of the original work.** If the work was made to make money and your reproductions infringe on that person's ability to make money then there is an infringement. If the origins of the work were more educational your case is sounder.
- **The amount and substantiality of the portion of the work used or reproduced, in relation to the size of the whole.** For purposes of criticism, pieces of literature are often quoted, and this should obviously be no more than necessary. For example; you can't quote a whole poem without permission, but you could quote a line as long as it was attributed.
- **The effect the use has on the potential market of the copyrighted work.** This considers if there is harm or potential harm caused to the market of the original work. This test takes into account the harm to the original and to derivative works. If you were to use a particular well-known product, trademark, or recognised part of a product still under copyright restrictions and present it in a negative way with, let's say, some negative political or social comments, you could be in infringement of copyright. This area is the stickiest as far as copyright law is concerned, and it's here that things still have to be defined. Criticism through reproduction and satire are obviously essential in countries where free speech is regarded as paramount, yet certain multi-nationals have used this clause to try to protect their products or name from artistic reproduction, satire and comment. Fortunately judges seem to have started to find in the artists' favour using the other clauses in the fair use legislation.

## WHAT DOES THIS MEAN TO THE ARTIST?

Copying someone else's work and pretending that it's your own idea and design is obviously unacceptable and recognised as such everywhere. Although this is often an area where the hurt party can do the least about it, someone can claim prejudice where they can prove that an object is a carbon copy of an original with dates and photos or a website or book inclusion to prove it. Only financial gain by the copier, financial prejudice to the copied person or legal copyrighting (this can be done through the internet) will result in a financial reward to the person who has been deliberately copied in such a way.

## IMAGES

If you copy something as a textile artist, an exact copy of another textile artist's work is obviously invalid practice, but you may wish to include other known images in your work, in which case you should use the guidelines above to decide if this is possible.

Generally speaking if you use a known or existing image from anywhere or anything and use the image 'mixed in' with your work, or reproduced in a different way from the original (embroidered instead of painted), you will be able to claim 'fair use', although this will depend on the factors cited above. For example, if you decide to reproduce faithfully in embroidery the work of a little known, but selling artist, without acknowledging where you copied it from, you should not be surprised if the artist is angry and takes steps to have your work destroyed. If you are simply 'inspired' by another work of art, yet acknowledge this inspiration, you will be enhancing the artist's reputation by calling attention to him or her, so arguably your work is without prejudice.

Obviously you can reproduce faithfully in embroidery or textile art techniques any image you like if you acknowledge the debt and do not do it for profit; if the author of the image has been dead for more than 75 years, then there can be no problem at all.

If you are using items from the commercial world around us, then the fourth clause has to be considered. It is arguable that with the draconian copyright laws that we now have, Andy Warhol would not have been able to create his Campell's Soup Cans, and of course Marilyn Monroe or her photographer would also have had a case. Most particularly, because Andy Warhol did do these pieces and they are considered to be worthy art with a huge dollar price ticket, lawyers have been able to fight and win for the artist's liberty of expression in relation to such 'found' images. Artists using or re-presenting such images in their work for comment and reconsideration do sometimes have to fight court battles; but this shouldn't put you off as it is unlikely to happen unless your work is very controversial and very widely exposed.

## THE PRINTED WORD

The reuse of the printed word or literary material in visual art pieces is generally accepted, on condition that acknowledgement is given, although, if you wish to reproduce a whole poem from a living author, you would be wise to ask for permission because of the notion of prejudice. The quotation of a piece of a poem with an acknowledgement could be seen as advantageous to the author, as people may well be inspired to seek out the poem to read the rest.

The use of books for altered books as an art process seems to be a widely accepted practice, although, if your altered book was then to be reproduced in its entirety, this could be considered prejudicial to the original, so you may wish to avoid this. Consider that a typographical layout of a book is copyrighted for 25 years after its first printing and this can help, or that the text itself is no longer in copyright after 70 years. If you don't have a particular personal reason for choosing and working into a more recent book, then it might just be as well to use only old volumes.

Copyright is a difficult subject even for judges and lawyers, and the law is often being tested, especially in relation to 'fair use' in current art practice. So, although the above is very important, please don't allow it to stop you from creating. The basic rule is, if you copy anything from another artist, acknowledge it and don't do a series of reproductions of someone else's product with the aim of making heaps of money – if the artist takes you to court you will lose it all!

# CONCLUSION

There aren't many things that can't be stitched onto or into, that can't be pieced with, coloured or glued on, that can't be bound wrapped or covered. It's enough to just look around and use what you have to hand and can find, then adapt it for a new, and possibly improved, use. Many of the basic ideas and 'recipes' included here could be adapted for all manner of things, so enjoy yourself and, above all, recycle.

# USEFUL ADDRESSES

**www.cjenkinscompany.com**

Inventors of bubble jet set 2000, a product for preparing fabrics for printing on an ink jet or bubble jet printer. You can also find good quality freezer paper and pre-prepared fabrics.

**www.Paverpol.nl**

Paverpol is a textiles hardener, perfectly safe to use, which hardens textiles, leather, paper, flowers and so on. It sticks to everything except plastic. The result can be used outdoors, but best not in humid conditions unless treated with the special varnish available in matt or satin finish. Or use Paverplast (100g per litre) to create pieces that remain watertight.

# GLOSSARY

**Adhesive webbing:** *A fusible webbing structure that is sticky on both sides when ironed. It is presented backed with a non sticky paper backing that is easily removed. It can be used to stick two fabrics surfaces together, or often to transfer paint or ink to fabric surfaces (often sold as Bondaweb).*

**Angelina fibres:** *Fine 15 denier synthetic fibres which fuse together when ironed.*

**Aquabond:** *A water soluble fabric of the same quality as Solusheet, but with a sticky side backed with paper. Dissolves in cold water, but much better in hot water or under a running tap.*

**Aquafilm:** *A dissolvable plastic film available in several types of thickness. The finest are best used just for topping or backing other materials for support. The thickest, or 'Romeo', can be stitched on out of a hoop and leaves a residue suitable for moulding when vanished in cold water.*

**Baking parchment:** *A silicone paper that is completely non-stick. It is frequently used to protect the iron or ironing board when heating surfaces that may stick. It's a useful habit to adopt whenever using surfaces that are a bit doubtful. Teflon paper can also be used. Both types of paper can be reused.*

**Cable stitch:** *Is worked when a thicker or more delicate thread is placed on the bobbin of the machine with the notion that the correct side of the work will be the underside where the bobbin thread shows. To achieve this, keep the top tension a little tight – between 5 and 6, and gradually loosen off the bobbin tension until the thicker thread will pull through without too much*

difficulty. *If the bobbin tension is too loose you will have bobbles of bobbin thread. If it is too tight, the top thread will be pulled through to the bottom in a reverse feather stitch. If it is just right you will be able to achieve a perfectly couched thread. If the bobbin tension is completely by-passed on a horizontal bobbin race machine, or on a vertical bobbin race machine with an open bobbin case, the result may have bobbles. Speed will count in the result – a faster machine speed will give fewer bobbles.*

**Colouring in:** *A term used for filling in an area with (usually) one colour, and usually in straight lines of machine running stitch, although other textures could be used.*

**Cotton linters:** *Partly processed cotton fibres sold in sheet form and suitable for paper making.*

**Crystal strands:** *synthetic fibres which fuse together when ironed – a little coarser than Angelina fibres*

**Feather stitch:** *Feather stitch is created by tightening the top tension and loosening the bobbin tension, or by-passing the tension spring in an open vertical bobbin case, or with a horizontal bobbin case. The thread should flow very easily through the bobbin case so that large loops of the bobbin thread appear on the surface of the work. When by-passing the tension the speed of working will have an effect. The slower the machine speed, the greater the loops.*

**Flax:** *Available as natural, bleached or dyed fibres as the source for linen. Spinner's waste can sometimes be obtained at specialist outlets (I found some in an eco-museum).*

**Fleece stitch:** *See illustration on page 9.*

**Heataway:** *A muslin type fabric that vanishes in dry heat such as under an iron, with a heat tool or in an oven.*

**Paintshop pro:** *A computer program used for manipulating images or photographs.*

**Pavapol:** *A fabric hardener – see chapters one and two for details of how to use.*

**Photoshop:** *A computer program used for manipulating images or photographs, available in amateur or professional formats.*

**PVA glue:** *A white glue, frequently used in the building industry, that dries perfectly clear (and stays this way). It can be used for gluing most absorbent surfaces together or for protecting or priming a surface.*

**Silk tops:** *Carded silk prepared for spinning into long fibre lengths.*

**Solusheet:** *Sometimes called Vylene Soluble. This is a firm non-woven fabric that dissolves in cold water, but more thoroughly and easily in warm water. Residue can be left in the work to stiffen it or even sculpt it. All residue can be removed through overnight soaking. Usually used in a hoop, it can undergo a great deal of embroidery without breaking up. See also Aquabond.*

**Stippling:** *This is a little like vermicelli stitch in that it works backwards and forwards in a wiggly movement but on a much greater scale, with much larger gaps between the stitching.*

**Throwster's waste:** *Short stranded filaments of silk that have passed through the spinner's (also known as throwster's) machine. Discarded unusable remnants are sold in their raw gummy state.*

**Topstitch needle:** *Similar to an Embroidery needle for a machine, but with an even longer hole, and so even easier to pass thicker threads, or indeed normal threads.*

**Vanishing paper:** *Paper that dissolves in cold water, but more easily if soaked in warm water.*

**Walking foot:** *Available for most machines that do not have an inbuilt dual feed. This foot, which actually has a walking motion, ensures that the top fabric is threaded through at the same speed as the bottom fabric. Useful for matching seams or stitching on quilted surfaces, it can also protect plastics, metals, leathers and other surfaces which may mark.*

**Whip stitch:** *The top tension is increased to pull the bobbin thread through to the top of the fabric. To help in this process the bobbin tension can also be loosened so that the top thread can pull the bobbin thread through more easily. The stitch should present loops that are less pronounced than in a feather stitch.*

**Wool tops:** *This is pre-carded wool ready for spinning, which has already been formed through a series of carding machines into a long continuous untwisted rope. The shorter fibres will have been removed by combing.*

# INDEX